THE
Acoustic Guitar

THE
Acoustic Guitar

Nick Freeth & Charles Alexander

COURAGE
BOOKS
AN IMPRINT OF RUNNING PRESS
PHILADELPHIA • LONDON

Nick Freeth

Nick Freeth was born in London in 1956. After graduating from St. Catharine's College, Cambridge with a degree in English Literature, he joined the BBC in 1978, and later became a senior producer in the World Service, where he specialized in making radio programs covering folk, jazz, and blues. Nick left the BBC in 1990 to work as Senior Producer for the London radio station Jazz FM, producing the 26-part series "100 Years of Jazz" and a wide range of other shows. In 1992, he was appointed Head of Music Production at Rewind Productions, an independent company making radio programs for the BBC; his credits there included series presented by Maddy Prior of Steeleye Span, and country music star Emmylou Harris. In 1994, Nick and Charles Alexander formed their own production company, Gleneagle Productions, whose recent BBC radio commissions have included a 12-part survey of "The Guitar in Jazz", and a series examining the history of jazz in Nazi Germany.

Nick is a self-taught guitarist, who has performed in a number of amateur bands in the London area, and enjoys listening to good playing in many different styles. Among his favorite guitarists are Ry Cooder, Jerry Garcia, John Fahey, and Derek Bailey.

Charles Alexander

An active jazz guitarist for over 30 years, Charles Alexander performs with several groups on the London jazz scene and is Jazz Guitar Tutor at Richmond Adult and Community College.

Born in Edinburgh, Scotland, Charles took up guitar at the age of 14, inspired by early rock 'n' roll, R & B, and the music of Django Reinhardt. He played his first gig at 15 on a Hofner bass guitar and later supplemented his student grant playing with local rock bands, dance bands, and jazz groups. In 1973 he moved to London to become Director of the Jazz Centre Society, a non-profitmaking organization that produced hundreds of jazz events ranging from weekly club gigs to full-scale festivals.

From 1980 to 1988 he was President of the International Jazz Federation. In 1984 he founded the company Jazzwise Publications, which markets printed jazz music and study materials and organizes jazz courses, including the Jamey Aebersold Jazz Summer School. He is publisher of the monthly *Jazzwise* magazine.

As a radio broadcaster, Charles wrote and presented the 12-part series "The Guitar in Jazz" for BBC Radio 3 and presented seven series of "Six Silver Strings" programs for BBC Radio 2, featuring a wide range of guitar music from classical to jazz, from blues to flamenco, and from Brazilian to country. He is a partner with co-author Nick Freeth in the independent radio production company Gleneagle Productions.

PHOTOGRAPHERS
Neil Sutherland & Don Eiler

COMMISSIONING EDITOR
Will Steeds

EDITOR
Philip de Ste. Croix

DESIGNER
Phil Clucas MSIAD

PRODUCTION
Neil Randles & Karen Staff

PRODUCTION DIRECTOR
Graeme Procter

PRINTED AND BOUND IN ITALY
New Interlitho Italia SpA

5041 The Acoustic Guitar

Created by CLB International,
Godalming, Surrey, England
Copyright ©1999 Quadrillion Publishing
Limited
First published in the United States in 1999 by
Running Press

9 8 7 6 5 4 3 2 1
Digit on the right indicates the number of this printing.

Library of Congress Cataloging-in-Publication Number 98-072522

ISBN 0-7624-0419-1

Published by Courage Books, an imprint of Running Press Book Publishers,
125 South Twenty-second Street, Philadelphia, Pennsylvania 19103-4399

Contents

Acknowledgements

The authors would like to thank the many luthiers, players, dealers, collectors, experts, and museums who have assisted them in the preparation of this book. Without their kindness and generosity, it would have been impossible to write it. Especial thanks go to Robert and Cindy Benedetto; Tony Bingham; Joshua Breakstone; Jimmy Bruno; John Buscarino; Doug Chandler, Chandler Guitars, Kew; Deanna Cross, The Metropolitan Museum of Art, New York; Dick Institute Art Gallery and Museum, Kilmarnock; Marie Gaines, McGregor Gaines and Don Young, National Reso-Phonic Guitars; Stephen Graham, editor of *Jazzwise* magazine; the staff of Hank's Guitar Shop, London; Richard Hoover, Santa Cruz Guitar Company; Stan Jay and the staff of Mandolin Brothers, New York; Dave Kelbie; Steve Klein, Klein Custom Guitars; Fapy Lapertin; Ben Levin and Chris Cobb, Real Guitars, San Francisco; Mark Makin; Chris Martin IV, Dick Boak, and John Wettlaufer, Martin Guitar Company; the manager and staff of McCabe's Guitar Shop, Santa Monica; Tim Miklaucic and Socrates Buenger, Guitar Salon International, Santa Monica; John Monteleone; Arnold Myers, Hon. Curator, Edinburgh University Collection of Historic Musical Instruments; Dr. Frances Palmer, Keeper of Musical Instruments, The Horniman Museum & Gardens; Dave Peabody; Alison Poulsen, Collections Associate, Autry Museum of Western Heritage, Los Angeles; Dale Rabiner; Andy Robinson; Eric Schoenberg; Nials Solberg; Gary Southwell; Anne Steinberg, Ashmolean Museum, Oxford; Craig Snyder; Bob Taylor and John D'Agostino, Taylor Guitars; Martin Taylor; Alan Timmins; Dale Unger, American Archtop Co.; Shel Urlik; Ray Ursell; Graham Wade; Mrs. Elizabeth Wells, Curator, Museum of Instruments, Royal College of Music, London; Stan Werbin, Elderly Instruments; Derrick Weskin.

We are also very grateful to the two indefatigable photographers who worked with us on this project: Neil Sutherland and Don Eiler.

The translation of the Remy Médard poem on page 21 comes from Philip J. Bone's book *The Guitar and Mandolin* (© Irene Bone, 1972), and is reproduced by kind permission of the copyright holder, and the publishers, Schott & Co. Ltd (London).

The translated quotation from Syntagma Musicum by Michael Praetorius on page 22 comes from Harvey Turnbull's book *The Guitar from the Renaissance to the Present Day* (© Harvey Turnbull 1974, 1976), and is reproduced by kind permission of the copyright holder, and the current publishers, The Bold Strummer Ltd.

The quotations from Julian Bream (page 30) and Fr. Juan Martínez Sirvent (page 41) are taken from José L.Romanillos' book *Antonio de Torres, Guitar Maker – His Life and Work* (© 1987 José L.Romanillos; Julian Bream's preface © 1987 Julian Bream), and are reproduced by kind permission of the copyright holders, and the current publishers, The Bold Strummer Ltd.

The quotation from the interview with Dave Peabody (page 140) comes from the December 1996/January 1997 issue of *Blueprint* magazine, and is reproduced by kind permission of Dave Peabody and the former editor of *Blueprint*, Scott Duncan.

COURTESY YAMAHA CORPORATION OF AMERICA; PHOTOGRAPH BY IWAN TANUMIJAYA

Foreword by Martin Taylor

Reading this book takes me back to my own early memories of gazing at guitars in brochures and shop windows. I started playing when I was four years old, but even before that, I remember my father ordering a Hofner President archtop from a mail-order catalog. I can still recall the excitement when my brother and I watched our father opening the case to reveal this beautiful instrument – and that was the beginning of my fascination with the guitar.

When I was a little older, I used to take the train up to the West End of London to look at the guitars in the shop windows. As a kid, I wasn't allowed to play any of them, but I used to pick up all the free manufacturers' catalogs, and head for Shaftesbury Avenue Fire Station, where my aunt was the cook. She'd make me a mug of tea and a plate of baked beans on toast, and I'd sit for hours looking and dreaming through those catalogs, many of them for Gibsons, Martins and other American guitars that were either difficult to obtain or very expensive in the British Isles.

Until quite recently, those major manufacturers dominated the guitar market. If you were a jazz player, you had to have a Gibson, and if you were a folk player, you'd almost automatically choose a Martin. But in the last few years, there's been a move towards the smaller independent makers, most of whom are players themselves, and have come into the business because of their love for the sound and the look of the instrument. Two of my own guitars, the Bill Barker model given to me by Ike Issacs on my 21st birthday, and my 1988 Robert Benedetto, are by leading independents, and going to makers like these for an instrument is a bit like going to Savile Row to order a made-to-measure suit. They'll build it to your specifications, and more and more players are now prepared to pay thousands of dollars for the result – even if the name on the headstock is less famous than those of the longest established companies.

This kind of close connection between maker and player has always been present in the classical guitar world, as you'll see from this book. But the recent growth in fine independent archtop and flat-top making is part of a wider upsurge of interest in acoustic guitars. The "Unplugged" TV concerts and recordings, and the current interest in traditional music, have played their parts, but maybe the key factor is the guitar's own versatility, and its ability to appeal to people with differing musical tastes, reasons for playing, and degrees of commitment. One of the great things about the guitar is that it can be played at lots of different levels. Just one aspect – a few chords or a blues scale – can go a long way, and yet there is so much to learn on the guitar that you can never master it.

I don't think there are many other musical instruments that can give so much pleasure in so many ways, whether you're a jazz player like me, a classical performer, an amateur musician, or just someone who enjoys looking at beautiful guitars in a book like this one. Whatever your interest, I think you'll find something here to please you.

Introduction

This book charts the evolution of the acoustic guitar from the sixteenth century to the present day. Our primary focus is on the instrument itself, although we also include some information about composers, players, and other figures who have had a significant influence on its development. We have been keen to place the guitar in its historical and social context, especially in Section One, which covers the pre-twentieth century period. It is easy to forget that early guitars, many of them museum pieces associated with archaic musical styles, often provided the popular repertoire of their day, and were once as actively used (though not as plentiful!) as Gibsons or Martins are today. We have done our best to bring these older instruments back to life for the reader, with contemporary accounts and quotations describing how and where they were played.

Sections Two and Three of the book cover the years from 1900 onwards, which have seen the emergence of several entirely new categories of guitar, as well as significant advances in design and technology. Most of these are discussed in the main text, but one topic – the use of electronic amplification – is mentioned here because of the problems it poses for anyone trying to define exactly what is (or is not) an "acoustic guitar." Many *bona fide* acoustic instruments, fully capable of being heard without amplifiers, now feature built-in pickups designed for onstage use; while some leading musicians, including the author of our Introduction, Martin Taylor, favor guitars that can provide both acoustic and electric sounds. Where do these hybrids fit in? And if a synthesizer-guitar player selects a digital sample of an acoustic when he performs, should his solid-bodied, MIDI-equipped instrument also be featured here?

After considerable thought and discussion, we have decided that, for the purposes of this book, any guitar, nylon- or steel-strung, can be considered an "acoustic" if it has been designed to provide a full and satisfactory sound without amplification. As a general rule, any fitted pickups should not compromise the acoustic tone by being mounted directly onto the instrument's top, although we have made very occasional exceptions to this. Our definition permits the inclusion of archtop guitars with "floating" magnetic pickups, as well as classical or flat-top models with piezo-electric "bugs" built into their bodies or bridge saddles. It excludes any solid or semi-solid designs, such as the MIDI controller mentioned earlier.

These rules have allowed us to feature a wide diversity of instruments – from classical and flamenco models to new and ingenious designs by leading luthiers on both sides of the Atlantic. We have endeavored to provide a representative cross-section of the very finest acoustic guitars, past and present, and we hope that this book will be as enjoyable to read as it was to research and write.

SECTION ONE
The Guitar's European Heritage

Despite their differences in size, pitch, and stringing, the earliest guitars, which appeared in Spain during the 1500s, shared some basic characteristics with their twentieth-century counterparts. Like today's instruments, they were versatile, portable, and suitable for simple playing styles as well as more elaborate music; and this widespread appeal was a key factor in establishing the primacy of the guitar over its rivals, the vihuela and lute.

The guitar's subsequent spread throughout Europe was aided by the activities of a number of widely-traveled composer/performers, one of the first of whom, Francesco Corbetta (1615–1681), helped to popularize it at the French and English courts. Later virtuosi, such as Fernando Sor (1778–1839) and Dionisio Aguado (1784–1849), made an even more direct impact on public tastes through their extensive concert tours. They also published music and instruction books, and were able to influence the development of the instrument itself through their recommendations and endorsements of individual makers. Gradually, the guitar, which had previously been subject to considerable local variations in construction and design, became more standardized; and by the late nineteenth century, larger, richer-sounding models of the type introduced by Antonio de Torres (1817–1892) and popularized by the player and composer Francisco Tárrega (1852–1909) had become the norm for concert use.

In this section, we trace the outline of the guitar's evolution throughout Europe, examining the work of the great Spanish, Italian, French, and German luthiers who laid the foundations for the instrument we know today. We also follow its progress in the New World, where émigré craftsmen such as C.F. Martin were soon to create a new, distinctively American version of the traditional design.

Chitarra battente by Giorgio Sellas, 1627. Standard guitars of this period were strung with gut and plucked with the fingertips. However, the model shown here, designed to provide chordal accompaniment to songs and dances, is fitted with wire strings and would have been played with a plectrum. Its front has mother-of-pearl and black mastic inlays; the sides and back are decorated with scrollwork and ivory inlays of nymphs and satyrs. (COURTESY ASHMOLEAN MUSEUM, OXFORD)

CHAPTER 1
THE GUITAR'S ORIGINS

Fretted, plucked instruments small enough to be held in the player's arms have existed, in Europe and elsewhere, for many centuries. Some of their names (chitarra, ghiterra) seem to suggest direct links with the modern guitar. Names, though, can be misleading, and while the terms used to classify musical instruments have changed little since the fourteenth and fifteenth centuries, their meanings are now frequently quite different. One musical theorist, Johannes Tinctoris, writing in Naples in about 1487, refers to a "ghiterra" or "ghiterna," which he says was invented by the Catalans – but this instrument, described by Tinctoris as "tortoise-shaped," is probably a round-backed lute rather than a guitar. However, Tinctoris also mentions a "viola without the bow," favored in Spain and Italy as an alternative to the lute; and it is this, not the ghiterra, which is almost certainly the direct ancestor of the guitar as we know it today.

"Viola" is an Italian word; its Spanish equivalent is "vihuela." In Renaissance Europe, the term covered a broad category of stringed instruments: some were played with a bow; others were held in the arms like a lute, and either struck with a pick, or plucked with the fingers of the hand. This third type (the "vihuela de mano") resembles the guitar most closely. Tinctoris says that, unlike the lute, it is "flat, and in most cases curved inwards on each side", suggesting the waisted, figure-of-eight shape now associated with the guitar. The vihuela de mano's strings were arranged in five or six pairs (or "courses") and the instrument may have been made in a number of different sizes; one surviving example in Paris is relatively large, and could have been designed to provide lower parts in ensembles and consorts.

By contrast, the earliest guitars, which probably emerged in Spain during the early 1500s, were smaller and higher-pitched, with four courses or groups of strings. None of them survive; but they are illustrated and described in a number of theoretical treatises, and in the collections of guitar music that began to appear in the second half of the sixteenth century. Guillaume Morlaye's book of songs and dances for the "guyterne" was published in Paris in 1552, and it was followed by other anthologies issued in Spain, England, and the Netherlands. Although one of these books refers to "the four-course vihuela, which is called guitar," and another contemporary source describes the guitar as "nothing but a vihuela shorn of its first and sixth strings," it seems clear that by this time, the guitar had developed its own independent identity and repertoire. Its restricted range made it well suited to simple dance-tunes and song accompaniment, while the vihuela excelled in more elaborate, contrapuntal music. The two instruments co-existed for a considerable period, but by the start of the seventeenth century, they were both being eclipsed by the growing appeal of the five-course guitar.

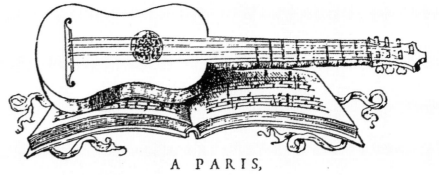

QVATRIESME LIVRE
CONTENANT PLVSIEVRS FANTASIES,
Chansons, Gaillardes, Paduanes, Branfles, reduictes en Tabulature de Guyterne,
& au ieu de la Cistre, par Maistre Guillaume Morlaye,
& autres bons autheurs.

A PARIS,
De l'imprimerie de Michel Fezandar, au mont fainct Hylaire, a l'hoftel d'Albret,
1552.
Auec priuilege du Roy, pour dix ans.

Above: The title page of Guillaume Morlaye's collection of music for the four-course guitar, which was published in Paris in 1552. The guitar in the illustration has a single top string, and double strings on its three remaining courses.

Above: *The title-page of* El Maestro, *a collection of music for the vihuela by the Spanish composer Luis Milán (c.1500–c.1561), published in 1536. It depicts the mythological poet and musician Orpheus in an idealized sylvan setting, playing a six-course vihuela. Despite the number of strings, the illustration shows only ten tuning pegs; similar small inaccuracies are found in many other artists' impressions of early instruments. The vihuela's neck, headstock, and outline all resemble those of a guitar.*

The Five-Course Guitar

The musical limitations of the four-course guitar were clear to sixteenth-century players and theorists. As early as 1555, the Spanish composer Juan Bermudo, in his "Libro primo de la declaración de instrumentos musicales," pointed out that its range could be extended "by adding…a string a fourth above the present first course". The oldest surviving five-course guitar, dating from 1581 and shown below, was one of the first instruments to put Bermudo's prescriptions into practice. It was probably tuned in a way corresponding to the intervals between the top five strings on a modern guitar – a system outlined in the Spanish scholar Miguel de Fuenllana's *Orphenica Lyra*, published in 1554.

Despite this superficial similarity, five-course guitars sounded very different from today's instruments. Their actual pitch was not standardized, but varied with individual guitars, string tolerances and musical needs. More significantly, the "bourdon" tunings used for the pairs of strings on some courses meant that notes assigned to these would be heard at both their fingered pitch, and an octave below. This created jangling doublings when chords were played, and allowed composers scope for a number of other effects that are difficult or impossible to reproduce on a guitar with six single strings.

Music for the five-course guitar was of two main types. The easiest style of playing to master was the simple strumming popularized by Juan Carlos Amat's *Guitarra Española de cinco órdenes*, first published in 1596. The year before, Francisco Palumbi had introduced a new system of naming chords for the guitar using letters of the alphabet. His approach, which was even simpler to learn than the numbers and tables used by Amat, became widely known in the early 1600s; and the "alfabeto" system remained in vogue all over Europe for the next 100 years.

Alongside this basic, popular style of playing, more elaborate and sophisticated works for the five-course guitar started to appear throughout the seventeenth century, as the instrument's popularity spread across Europe. Most of these were created by professional court musicians, whose patrons could afford the finest performers, teachers, and instruments. In the next few pages, we examine the impact of one of the most important of these figures, Francesco Corbetta, and a few of his contemporaries, and also look at some of the finest guitars made outside Spain during this period.

Left, above, and below: *The top, side, and back of an elaborately decorated guitar, probably made in Italy around 1630, and later extensively altered.* (COURTESY EDINBURGH UNIVERSITY)

The top is made from a pine-type wood, and the illustrations of exotic animals, birds and plants are carved from ebony and ivory. The neck and six-string headstock are not original.

Above: *The earliest five-course guitar still in existence. It was made by Belchior Diaz in Lisbon, and is dated December 1581. It is relatively small – only 30in (76.5cm) long – and its open soundhole would originally have contained a "rose." Its bridge and belly are later additions, but its neck, headstock, sides, and back are all original.*

(COURTESY ROYAL COLLEGE OF MUSIC, LONDON)

The Seventeenth-Century Guitar in Europe

The "alfabeto" chordal system caught on quite quickly in early seventeenth-century Italy, creating a considerable demand there for instruments and music to play on them. Makers of lutes soon began to build guitars for this thriving new market, and among the leading craftsmen of the period were the Sellas family (notably Matteo and Giorgio), whose three Venice workshops produced many fine five-course guitars. Some surviving examples of these (including, probably, the Sellas instrument shown below) have been converted to "chitarre battenti" – wire-strung guitars designed specifically for strumming dance rhythms and song accompaniments, and played with a pick.

Gradually, a demand developed in Italy for more complex guitar compositions, and "alfabeto"-type symbols were combined with other forms of printed tablature capable of

showing melodies and inner parts as well as simple chords (standard staff notation was not used for the guitar until the eighteenth century). Among the early pioneers of this more substantial music was Giovanni Paolo Foscarini (d. 1649), a lutenist as well as a guitar player, whose compositions combined straightforward strumming with lute-like "pizzicati." Even more influential was Francesco Corbetta (1615–1681), whose first published music appeared in 1639, about ten years after Foscarini's. Corbetta traveled widely throughout Europe: after initial success as a virtuoso guitar player, composer, and teacher in Italy, he visited Spain, enjoying the patronage of King Philip IV, and went on to play a significant role in popularizing the guitar throughout Europe – and especially in France and England.

Below right and opposite page: *A five-course guitar built, in the Venetian style, by Jacobo Checchucci of Livorno in 1628.*

(COURTESY TONY BINGHAM)

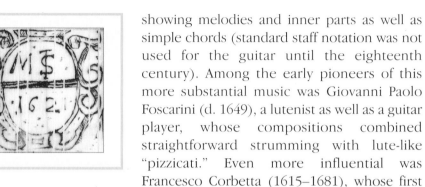

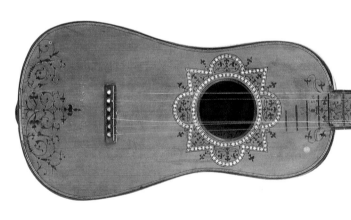

Above: *Chitarra battente by Matteo Sellas, 1638. The table is pine with a pin-style bridge, which is a nineteenth-century replacement for the original.*

(COURTESY THE DICK INSTITUTE, KILMARNOCK)

Below: *The headstock for this instrument carries the maker's inscription "Matteo Sellas alla Corona in Venetia 1638." Beneath this, extending down the fingerboard, are a series of six ivory plaques engraved with a stag, a bear, a camel, a fox with a goose, a hare, and a hound. The guitar's table is made from pine, inlaid at the base and the neck joint with ebony.*

(COURTESY THE DICK INSTITUTE, KILMARNOCK)

Right and inset (left): A chitarra battente made by Magno Stregher in Venice in 1621. Its table is profusely inlaid with ivory, ebony, and mother-of-pearl. The headstock and fingerboard are also beautifully decorated, and Stregher's initials and the date are visible at the base of the fingerboard.

(COURTESY THE DICK INSTITUTE, KILMARNOCK)

The Influence of Francesco Corbetta

Francesco Corbetta first came to Paris in the mid-1650s, when Louis XIV (who had acceded to the French throne in 1643) was still a teenager. Over the following decades, French guitar music and its composers became a dominant influence throughout Northern Europe, and the popularity of Corbetta's performances, compositions, and teaching at the French court played a key role in bringing this about. However, the guitar had already been firmly established in France since the sixteenth century, and there was a long tradition of fretted instrument making in Paris and other centers. The most distinguished heirs to this tradition were the Voboam family – René, Jean, and Alexandre. Their reputations as craftsmen must have been well known to the King, who was himself a keen guitarist; and at least two instruments by Jean Voboam were owned and played by Louis' daughters.

Voboam instruments also found their way to England, and Corbetta's first visit there, in 1662, soon created the same enthusiasm for the guitar at Charles II's court in London as already existed at Louis' court at Versailles. A contemporary observer commented that "the liking expressed by the King for [Corbetta's] compositions had made this instrument so fashionable that everyone was playing it – well or badly. Even on the dressing tables of all the beauties one could rely on seeing a guitar as well as rouge and beauty spots."

Corbetta returned to France in about 1670, and continued to play, teach, and compose for the last 11 years of his life. Among his many pupils was the leading figure of the next generation of French guitar composers, Robert de Visée (c.1660–c.1720), some of whose music still remains in today's classical

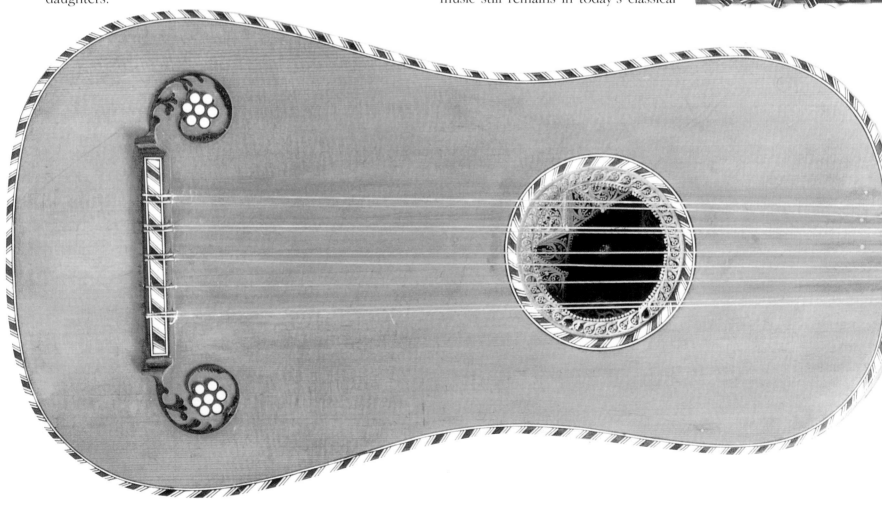

guitar repertoire. Corbetta died in Paris in 1681: this touching tribute is said to have been written by another of his distinguished students, the guitarist and composer Remy Médard.

> *"Ci-git l'Amphion de nos jours*
> *Francisque, cet homme si rare,*
> *Qui fit parler a la guitare*
> *Le vrai language des amours."*

> *(Here lies the Amphion of our days,*
> *Francis Corbet, this man of rare quality,*
> *Who made his guitar speak*
> *The very language of love's jollity.)*

(TRANSLATION BY PHILIP J. BONE)

Left and bottom of page: *This guitar has a colorful legend attached to it: it is said to have been given by Mary, Queen of Scots (1542–1587), to her Italian-born private secretary, David Rizzio, who was murdered at Holyrood House, Edinburgh, in 1566. However, the instrument's design and appearance make it much more likely to be a French guitar dating from around the 1680s. It was probably made in Paris by Jean Voboam.*

(COURTESY ROYAL COLLEGE OF MUSIC, LONDON)

Left and above right: *A five-course guitar made by René Voboam in Paris in 1641. The table is spruce, and the back and sides are tortoiseshell, with ebony and ivory inlays. The binding around the edge of the body and the fingerboard is also ebony and ivory, as are the bridge, soundhole, and fingerboard decorations.*

(COURTESY ASHMOLEAN MUSEUM, OXFORD)

21

The Work of Stradivari, Tielke, and Vieyra

Corbetta's reputation helped to promote wide interest in the guitar throughout Europe. He, Foscarini, and others had begun to create a substantial repertoire for the instrument, giving it a musical respectability it had lacked in the days when it was associated only with simple strumming. This frivolous image was long established and took many years to dispel. In Spain, the guitar had developed strong links with taverns, barbers' shops, and playhouses; and in 1619, the leading German musical historian and composer Michael Praetorius (1571–1621) described it as "used in Italy by…comedians and buffoons only for accompaniment to Villanelles and other foolish low songs." Despite these comments, there was enough serious demand for the instrument in seventeenth-century Germany to support an important center of guitar making in Hamburg. Its founder was Hans Christoph Fleischer, whose son-in-law, Joachim Tielke (1641–1719), later became recognized as one of the finest luthiers in Europe.

Another sign of the instrument's growing acceptance in serious musical circles was the fact that the most celebrated of all stringed instrument makers, Antonio Stradivari (1644–1737) of Cremona in Italy, began to make guitars in the second part of the seventeenth century. Only four complete examples of these survive; the one shown below is in the Ashmolean Museum in Oxford, and there is another five-course Stradivari in the Paris Conservatoire National.

Practically no Spanish guitars from this period are still in existence, and the final guitar shown here is one of the few surviving Portuguese instruments from the late seventeenth century. It is unusual in having six courses – anticipating one of the many important modifications to the guitar's construction that would start to take place in the following 100 years.

Above: *Five-course guitar attributed to Jakob Stadler of Munich, c.1625*
(COURTESY ROYAL COLLEGE OF MUSIC, LONDON)

Above left:
A five-course guitar built by Antonio Stradivari in 1688. Its table is spruce; the head, neck, sides, and back are maple, with ebony inlays.
(COURTESY ASHMOLEAN MUSEUM, OXFORD)

Above left and above right: *A six-course guitar, made by Santos Vieyra in Portugal at the end of the seventeenth century.* (COURTESY ASHMOLEAN MUSEUM, OXFORD)

Below: *A late seventeenth-century five-course guitar by Joachim Tielke of Hamburg.* (COURTESY ROYAL COLLEGE OF MUSIC, LONDON)

23

CHAPTER 2
THE GUITAR: 1700–1900

During the eighteenth century, guitar bodies became larger, their internal bracing underwent radical improvements, and their stringing patterns began to change – from five to six courses (the six-course instrument was popular in Spain from the 1780s to the early 1800s, but failed to catch on elsewhere), and eventually to the modern system of six single strings.

These changes took place gradually, with different styles of guitar co-existing for many years. Some early eighteenth-century instruments were subsequently modified to take the new string configurations. The French guitar shown opposite originally had five courses; these have been replaced with six strings, and the fingerboard, metal frets, headstock, and bridge are all subsequent additions. The elaborate parchment rose is part of the original design; it was soon to become less common, as more and more eighteenth-century luthiers began to build guitars with open soundholes.

The design of the soundboard was also under scrutiny. Until the latter part of the century, guitar tops, whose vibrations play a crucial role in creating the sound of an instrument, were light and thin in construction, with little internal support to help them withstand the constant pressure from the strings. This often resulted in the kind of cracking and warping visible in the photograph of the "Zaniboni" guitar on page 25. The problem of providing adequate bracing for guitar soundboards, while still allowing them to vibrate efficiently, was solved by the use of "fan-bracing," which involved gluing wooden struts onto the back of the soundboard in outwardly radiating patterns. The earliest maker known to have done this was Francisco Sanguino of Seville, whose first fan-braced guitar, made in 1759, is in the Gemeente-museum in the Hague. Other luthiers associated with the development of fan-bracing included Juan Pagés (d. 1821) and José Benedid (1760–1836) of Cádiz. The system was copied and adapted by later craftsmen, and

eventually refined and perfected by the great nineteenth-century Spanish guitar maker Antonio de Torres (1817–1892).

The eighteenth century also saw changes to the neck, headstock, and bridge. Gut frets gradually disappeared, to be replaced with metal ones permanently inlaid into the fingerboard. Geared machine heads began to be used instead of wooden tuning pegs; while bridges were fitted with ivory or bone saddles, and sometimes had pins to hold down the string ends. (Pin-style bridges continued to be used on gut-strung guitars throughout the nineteenth century, and later became standard on flat-top steel-strung guitars.)

In the following pages we will look at a cross-section of guitars from early 1700s to 1840, and trace the introduction of some of these developments. However, we begin by examining the range of playing styles that provided the basis for the instrument's ongoing popularity during this period.

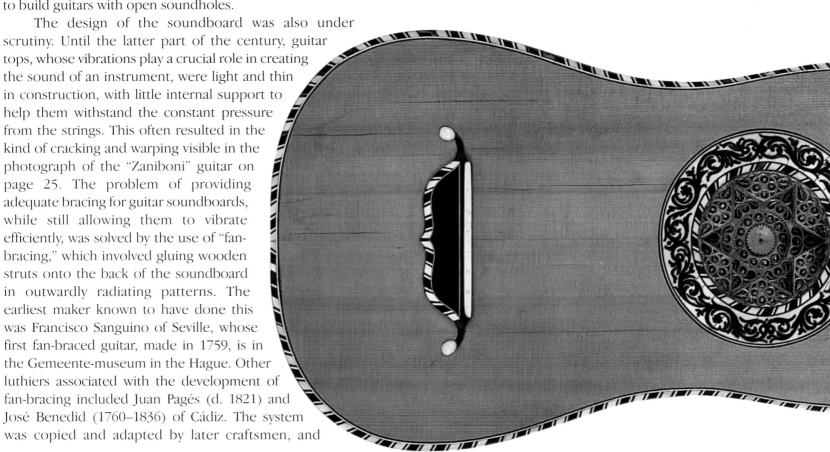

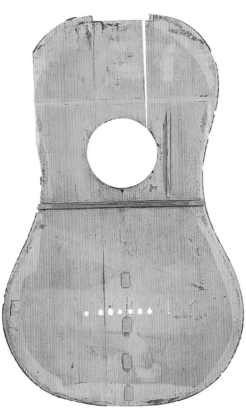
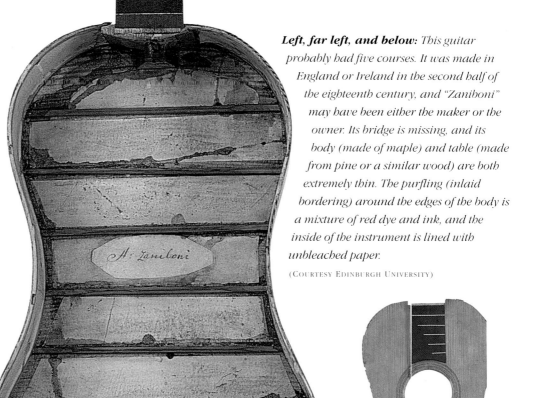

Left, far left, and below: *This guitar probably had five courses. It was made in England or Ireland in the second half of the eighteenth century, and "Zaniboni" may have been either the maker or the owner. Its bridge is missing, and its body (made of maple) and table (made from pine or a similar wood) are both extremely thin. The purfling (inlaid bordering) around the edges of the body is a mixture of red dye and ink, and the inside of the instrument is lined with unbleached paper.*

(COURTESY EDINBURGH UNIVERSITY)

Below and below right: *A French guitar made in the early 1700s, and attributed to a member of the Voboam family. It has been converted from five courses to six strings, and has also been fitted with machine heads, metal frets, and a pin bridge.*

(COURTESY EDINBURGH UNIVERSITY)

Playing Styles and Techniques

By the early 1700s, the guitar had largely replaced the lute as the favored instrument in royal courts and noble households. Francesco Corbetta and later player/composers such as Gaspar Sanz (1640–1710) provided their aristocratic patrons with melodious, refined music that made use of two contrasting ways of playing: the rasgueado or strumming style that had been associated with the guitar since the 1500s; and the punteado or plucked method that allowed the performance of more elaborate, contrapuntal works.

Punteado was a development of earlier vihuela and lute technique, in which the right-hand thumb and fingers are used independently to strike the strings. Its establishment led even

the guitar's detractors to recognize the instrument's musical capabilities. One of these was William Turner (1651–1739?), an Englishman who had served Charles II as "musician in ordinary in his Majesty's private Musick for lute and Voyce." Turner commented scornfully in 1697 that "the fine easie Ghittar, whose performance is soon gained, at least after the brushing way [*rasgueado*], hath at this present time over-topt the nobler lute" – but also admitted that "after the pinching way [*punteado*], the Ghittar makes some good work."

The increasing acceptance of the guitar as a "serious" instrument was mirrored by its continuing success at street level, as the disdain once expressed by some educated listeners for the popular side of its musical character began to

These pages: Five-course French or Belgian guitar, mid-eighteenth century. This instrument, which has a pine top, is inlaid with ebony, ivory, mother-of-pearl, and tortoiseshell, and its soundhole contains a three-tier rose made from vellum.

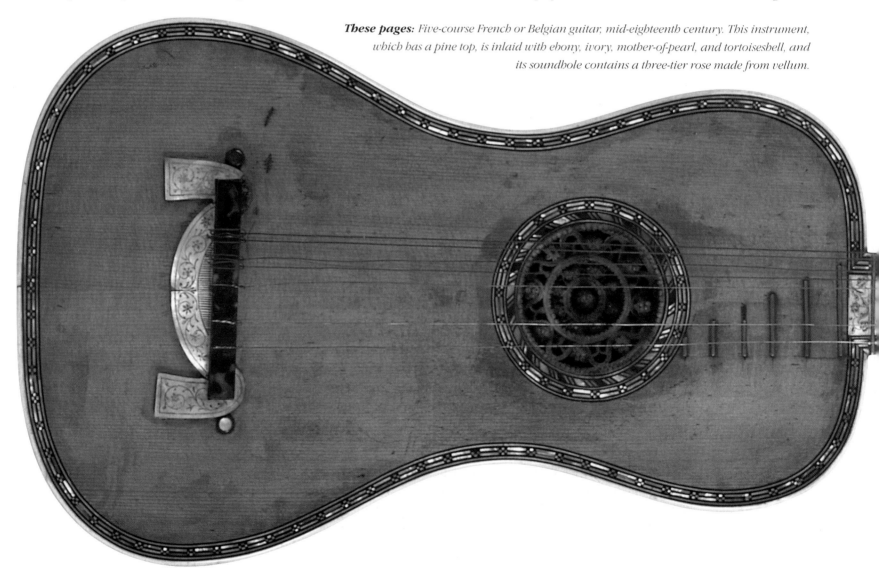

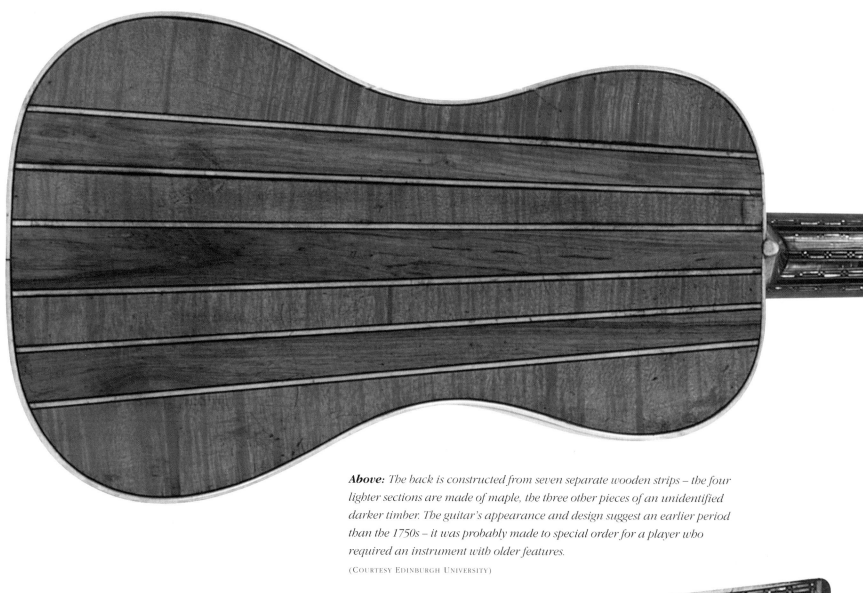

Above: The back is constructed from seven separate wooden strips – the four lighter sections are made of maple, the three other pieces of an unidentified darker timber. The guitar's appearance and design suggest an earlier period than the 1750s – it was probably made to special order for a player who required an instrument with older features.

(COURTESY EDINBURGH UNIVERSITY)

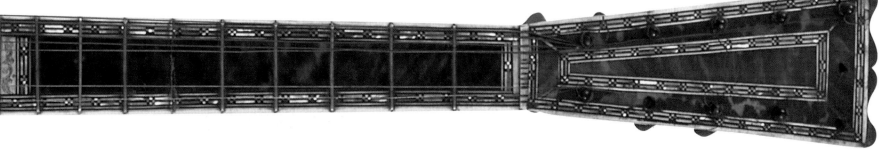

give way to appreciation and admiration. One French critic, François Raguenet, wrote in 1702 about the itinerant guitarists and violinists he heard performing in the streets of Rome, "accompanying their voices so justly that we seldom meet with much better music in our French consorts." His comments were echoed by later travelers; in the 1770s, the English musician, Dr. Charles Burney, enjoyed outdoor performances by peasant guitarists playing "a very singular species of music" in Naples and on the Piazza di San Marco in Venice, featuring "sometimes a single voice and guitar, and sometimes two or three guitars together." Traditional performing styles such as these had a perennial appeal, and played an important part in sustaining the guitar's vitality throughout the eighteenth and nineteenth centuries.

The Evolving Guitar

The five-course guitar stayed in vogue for much of the eighteenth century. Large quantities of music and tutors continued to be published for it, and it remained a favorite at many European royal courts. However, even some of its finest players acknowledged its deficiencies – especially in the bass range. In the early 1700s, the great French guitarist and composer Robert de Visée (c.1660 –c.1720), who was Francesco Corbetta's pupil, and subsequently became Louis XIV's personal guitar teacher, observed that his own guitar music had unavoidable weaknesses in its part-writing, adding that "the instrument itself" was the reason for this. Despite such comments, no fundamental changes were made to the guitar's range and number of strings for several decades, and the two instruments shown here were tuned and played in exactly the same way as their seventeenth-century predecessors.

This guitar in the main picture was probably made in about 1730 by the Venetian luthier Santa Serafin. Compared to the richly decorated instruments from Venice shown in Chapter 1, it is more restrained and functional in appearance, and also has a narrower waist, a flat back (theirs were rounded), and a slightly smaller overall body size. It was restored by Andrew Dipper in 1985; guitars of this period, with their lightweight construction, are particularly prone to damage, and relatively few have survived intact.

Andrew Dipper was also responsible for the restoration of the five-course guitar shown opposite, which was made by José Massaguer (1690–1764) in Barcelona in about 1750. In some ways, it seems more of a throwback to the previous century

Above: *A guitar by José Massaguer, Barcelona, c.1750. The soundboard is made from fir, the back from flamed maple. The pattern of the rosewood inlay beneath the bridge is balanced by a similar design on the upper fingerboard (above the 8th fret), and the wavy inlay along the rest of the neck and headstock is bordered with strips of ebony.*
(COURTESY METROPOLITAN MUSEUM OF ART, NEW YORK)

Left and below left: *A guitar attributed to Santa Serafin, Venice, c.1730. Its table is made of pine or a similar wood, edged with ebony and ivory. The only other body inlay is the soundhole decoration – a combination of purfling and circles of contrasting woods.*
(COURTESY EDINBURGH UNIVERSITY)

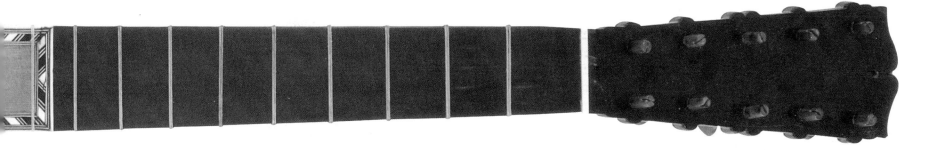

than the Italian instrument – although many other guitars of this period (especially Spanish ones) include "older" design features like the soundhole rose and elaborate body inlays seen here. Massaguer also made violins and other stringed instruments; only three other examples of his work are known to be still in existence.

Above: *The nut is ivory, and the fruitwood headstock is in a fan shape, with black inlays and tuning pegs of boxwood.*

Bertet and Fabricatore

The guitar shown below, made by the Paris-based luthier Bertet in 1766, retains many features familiar from older instruments. Its soundboard is relatively unadorned, with Bertet's name stamped near the bottom edge. Gut frets and a soundhole rose are still used, but the back, made from strips of maple and walnut, is flat, and the fingerboard completely plain.

Only about 15 years after this guitar was built, the first six-string instruments (the extra string extended their bass range by a fourth) began to appear in many European countries. Except in Spain, where guitars with six double courses of strings were common until the early nineteenth century, these new designs were all single-strung. The most likely reason for the change is that pairs of strings using bourdons or "re-entrant" tunings were becoming increasingly unsuitable for the music of the time. Julian Bream has described the five- and six-course guitar as "an admirable instrument particularly for songs and dances of a light, frothy character. Its ranks of paired strings, and characteristic split octave bass tuning, could produce a rash of wild harmonies and inverted counterpoint with a charm all its own." For classical and romantic music, these qualities were unwanted, and many composers and players would have welcomed the six-string's greater precision and depth of tone.

One of the leading early builders of six-string instruments was Giovanni Battista Fabricatore of Naples, whose first known guitar of this type was made in 1798. The guitar illustrated is a slightly later example of his work, from about 1805.

Below and below right: A five-course guitar by Bertet, built in 1766. The luthier's name and the inscription "A PARIS" are branded onto the instrument's table; at this period, Bertet's workshop was near the Comédie Française. (COURTESY TONY BINGHAM)

Top left: *A six-string guitar by Fabricatore, made in c.1805. Its soundboard is pine, and its fingerboard extends all the way down to the soundhole, as on most modern guitars. (Compare the Bertet guitar, the fingerboard of which ends well before the neck joins the body.) The soundhole and bridge are decorated with a combination of mother-of-pearl and red wax, and the same material is used for the purfling around the edge of the table and fingerboard.*

(COURTESY EDINBURGH UNIVERSITY)

The Guitar Virtuosi

The early history of the six-string guitar is dominated by the careers and influence of a handful of Spanish and Italian virtuosi, who established international reputations with their playing and compositions, and inspired a wave of interest in the guitar throughout Europe. The first of these players to become well-known outside his own country was Mauro Giuliani (1781–1829), who was born in Bologna, but achieved his first major success in Vienna, and later had an English guitar magazine (*The Giulianiad*, published from 1833) named in his memory.

Paris was a city with an even greater appeal to visiting guitarists, many of whom eventually made their homes there. Ferdinando Carulli (1770–1841) was born in Naples, and settled in the French capital in 1808; he was joined there five years later by the celebrated Spanish player and composer, Fernando Sor (1778–1839), and, in the 1820s, by two other famous names: Matteo Carcassi (1792–1853) and Dionisio Aguado (1784–1849).

Above and details: A guitar by Charles Lété, made in 1840. The inlays are mother-of-pearl, and the machine heads brass and ivory.

(COURTESY TONY BINGHAM)

This musical activity led to an upsurge in guitar-making throughout France, and both instruments shown here were built there during the height of the instrument's popularity. The guitar on the opposite page dates from the early years of the nineteenth century. It was made by Dubois of Paris, and was subsequently modified to take a seventh string – but has now been restored to its original condition.

The other guitar shown here is a beautiful instrument, made around 1840 by Charles Lété. Lété's workshop was in Mirecourt, a small town near Nancy in eastern France. The instrument's body is partly built of satinwood, an exotic timber from which Matteo Carcassi also had a guitar made at about

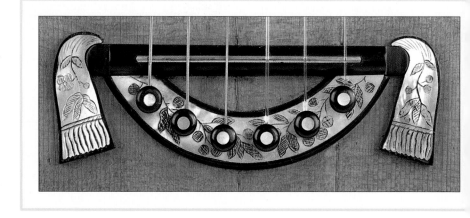

this time. Despite their exquisite workmanship, such highly-decorated models were soon to fall out of favor with more serious players; one leading guitar historian, Graham Wade, has described them in his book *Traditions of the Classical Guitar* as "caught in the evolutionary process between ornamented *objets d'art* and genuine musical instruments."

Bottom of page: *A guitar by Dubois, made in Paris during the early nineteenth century. It has ebony and mother-of-pearl purfling (in a chevron pattern) around its table, upper neck, and soundhole. There are also mother-of-pearl dots on the string pins and the edges of the "mustache" bridge. The body is made from pine and rosewood.*

(Courtesy Edinburgh University)

Sor's Choice

The popularity of the guitar led to a ready market for good-quality instruments throughout the musical centers of nineteenth-century Europe. There was also a lively debate among professionals and the public about the relative merits of guitars from different countries. Instruments from Spain were often proclaimed to be the finest, although some virtuosi had vested interests in promoting guitars made in other places. The Italian player Luigi Legnani (1790–1877), for example, was one of the first musicians to endorse a specific make of instrument; in the 1820s, guitars bearing his name were made and sold by two Viennese luthiers, Johann Georg Stauffer and Georg Ries.

Perhaps the most useful and disinterested views on the subject of choosing a fine guitar were those of the great Spanish player and composer Fernando Sor, writing in the short-lived English guitar magazine, *The Giulianiad,* in 1833: "The manner of constructing the body of the instrument is almost everywhere understood extremely well, and most Neapolitan, German and French guitars leave, in this respect, very little superiority to the Spanish. In the goodness of the body or box, the Neapolitans long surpassed, in my opinion, those of France and Germany; but that is not the case at present; and if I wanted an instrument, I would procure it…from M. Lacôte, a French maker, the only person who, besides his talents, has proved to me that he possesses the quality of not being inflexible to reasoning."

Sor goes on to praise the work of (among others) Alonzo of Madrid, and Pagés and Benedid of Cádiz; but modesty or scruples prevent him from mentioning the London-based luthier Louis Panormo (1784–1862), who consulted Sor on instrument design, used fan-bracing on his soundboards, and proudly proclaimed himself "London's only Maker of Guitars in the Spanish Style."

Oposite page and above: *A six-course guitar by José Pagés of Cadiz, made in 1813 – by which time paired stringing had largely fallen out of use. Its elaborate design, with ebony and mother-of-pearl inlays on the table and fingerboard, suggests that this was probably a "presentation" instrument, made to demonstrate the luthier's skill.*
(COURTESY EDINBURGH UNIVERSITY)

Left: *René François Lacôte (1785–1855), who had his premises at No. 10, Rue de Savoie, Paris, was acknowledged as the leading French luthier of his time. This guitar dates from 1825.*
(COURTESY HORNIMAN MUSEUM)

Right: *Guitar "in the Spanish style" by Louis Panormo, 1838. The Panormo family were Italian émigrés who settled in London.*
(COURTESY TONY BINGHAM)

Hybrids and Curiosities

Alongside musicians such as Sor, who encouraged guitar makers to refine and improve the quality of the regular six-string instrument, there were other players, luthiers, and inventors with more radical ideas. Some of them developed multi-stringed variants of the guitar, most of which had two (or more) necks, were difficult to tune and unwieldy to play, and did not survive for long. Other hybrid instruments were intended as a fusion of ancient designs and modern craftsmanship; the "lyre-guitar" is one example of this. Modeled on classical Greek lines, it was introduced at the end of the eighteenth century, and, with its six single strings and extended bass range, was intended as an improvement upon what one commentator described as the "primitive" five-course guitar. Despite the appearance of a few other similar models in the early 1800s, the lyre-guitar was not a great success.

A number of eminent nineteenth-century guitarists had distinctive instruments made to their own special designs – and one leading French player with particularly unusual requirements was a former pupil of Sor, Napoléon Coste (1806–1883). Coste commissioned the guitar shown below from the Paris luthier René Lacôte; it was probably made in the early 1840s. It has seven strings, an extra-large body, and was tuned a fifth lower than normal. Also remarkable are the massive bridge and tailpiece, and the elevated finger-rest at the side of the soundhole. Another of Coste's guitars can be seen at the museum of the Paris Conservatoire.

The final guitar shown here is an experimental model by Louis Panormo, built in 1831. In his London workshop at 46 High Street, Bloomsbury, Panormo offered "guitars of every description from 2 to 15 guineas," and this curiously shaped instrument is proof of the continuing lack of standardization in guitar design during the early decades of the nineteenth century. Although some guitars made in the first half of the nineteenth century bear an increasing resemblance to modern "classical" instruments, their shape and size was not finally settled until the advent of Torres in the 1860s.

Below: A "heptachord" made to Napoléon Coste's specifications by René Lacôte in Paris, c.1840.

(COURTESY TONY BINGHAM)

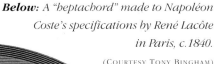

Opposite page, above left:
Experimental, oval-shaped guitar by Louis Panormo, London, 1831.

(COURTESY TONY BINGHAM)

Left: *The Louis Panormo guitar has a rosewood body and is decorated with ivory and mother-of-pearl inlays.*

Right: *Clementi and Company of London made this lyre-guitar in about 1800. The body is decorated in black lacquer with gilt arabesques, the upper arms feature a floral motif, and a female mask surmounts the head.*

Mrs. Sidney Pratten's Guitars

Virtuosi such as Sor, Aguado, Carcassi, and Carulli made an immense impact on the concert-going public, and all four men wrote detailed guitar methods that sold in their thousands to amateur players eager to master the instrument for themselves. But a large number of budding guitarists set their sights at a more modest level, hoping to gain just enough knowledge of the instrument to use their skills as a social asset. It was at this sizeable public that England's foremost teacher and popularizer of the guitar in the Victorian era, Mrs. Sidney Pratten, aimed most of her work.

Mrs. Pratten (Catherina Josepha Pelzer), was born in Mulheim, on the Rhine, in 1821. She was the daughter of a leading German guitarist, Ferdinand Pelzer (1801–1860), who taught her to play the instrument from an early age. Catherina made her London concert debut at the age of about nine; soon afterwards, the Pelzers left Germany to settle in England, and she quickly built up an outstanding reputation as a soloist. As a young woman, she began to teach the guitar in fashionable and aristocratic circles, and in 1854 she married an English flautist, Robert Sidney Pratten.

Above: A contemporary portrait of Mrs. Sidney Pratten (1821–1895). She had a distinguished career as a performer, and later became an influential teacher of the guitar in London.

Some years later, Mrs. Pratten published a comprehensive method for guitar, drawing on the work of Giuliani and Sor; but, as one of her friends later wrote, "[she] found…that the amateur pupil was not inclined to devote sufficient study to the instrument to gain the necessary technique to grapple with the difficulties of the music of the classic authors for the guitar." Her solution to this was a book entitled *Learning the Guitar Simplified by Mme. Sidney Pratten*, a mixture of elementary exercises and "pleasing pieces and Songs." It was a huge success, and had been through 12 editions at the time of her death in 1895.

As a leading player and teacher, Mrs. Pratten owned some fine nineteenth-century guitars, and some of these (which may have been made to her specifications) are shown here.

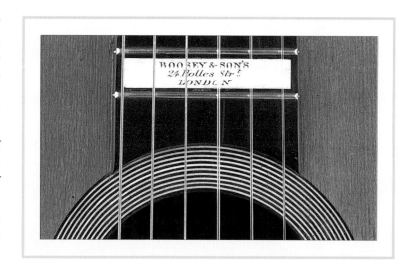

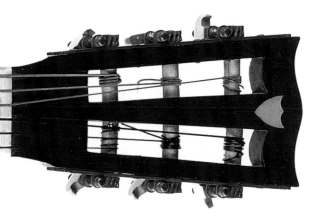

Above and below left: *Another French guitar, with an ivory plaque bearing the name of Boosey and Sons, who were already well-established as musical instrument retailers in London. The original label inside the soundhole carries Mrs. Pratten's signature, and is dated July 2, 1859.*

Left: *This richly inlaid guitar was made in France in about 1850, and imported by a London company, Addison and Hodson. Mrs. Pratten used a photograph of herself playing this instrument on her visiting card.*

Left: *A "bambino" guitar, designed for children, and owned by Mrs. Pratten. It was made in 1870 and is shown here with its original case.*

(ALL GUITARS ON THIS PAGE COURTESY TONY BINGHAM)

The Carpenter from Almería

The importance of Antonio de Torres in the development of the guitar is hard to overstate. A gifted craftsman, who was also a fine player, his designs took the achievements of previous luthiers to new levels of refinement and sophistication, and many aspects of his approach have become de facto standards for his successors.

Torres was born in 1817 at La Cañada de San Urbino, just outside Almería in southern Spain. After a brief spell as a conscript soldier, he married in 1835, and began his working career as a carpenter in the nearby village of Vera. There, he was dogged by financial worries and family tragedy; two of his three daughters died in infancy, and following the death of his wife (aged 23), he left the area and settled in Seville.

Below: This guitar was built by Antonio de Torres in Almería in 1882. It has a spruce top, back and sides of cypress, and a French polish finish.

It is not known exactly when Torres began making guitars, but he must have found the atmosphere of Seville a congenial place to develop his craft. The city had a thriving community of luthiers, and also attracted many leading players – among them Julián Arcas (1832–1882), who bought one of Torres' instruments, and encouraged him to become a full-time guitar builder. Torres followed this advice, and between 1856 and 1869 succeeded in establishing himself as the foremost luthier of his day – winning a medal at Seville's "Esposicion Agricola, Industrial y Artistica," and gaining commissions from a number of eminent clients – notably Francisco Tárrega (1852–1909).

Torres remarried in 1868; he had lived with his new wife, Josefa Martín Rosado, for a number of years previously. In 1869 he left Seville, gave up guitar-making, and used some of his wife's capital to open a china-shop in his home town of Almería. Despite the endorsement of Tárrega and other virtuosi, it appears that the income from building guitars was insufficient (or too uncertain) for the needs of Torres' family. He eventually returned to his craft as a part-time activity, working at his home, 20 Calle Real, La Cañada, where he and

his family also took in lodgers to help make ends meet. After the death of his second wife in 1883, he produced an increasing number of instruments, and by the time of his death in 1892, at the age of 75, he had made over 155 guitars.

Torres employed no assistants or apprentices, and his working methods were a carefully-guarded secret. His biographer, José Romanillos, has discovered and translated a fascinating account of his later life written by a local priest, Fr. Juan Martínez Sirvent, who was a close friend of the luthier. According to this, when performing critical tasks like gluing ribs, tops, and backs, "he always shut and locked the door of his workshop…so that no one could see him, not even his most intimate relatives." However, it seems unlikely that even the acutest observer could have discovered the key to Torres' genius simply by watching him. As he explained to Sirvent: "It is impossible to leave [my] secret behind for posterity; this will go to the tomb with me, for it is the result of the feel of the tips of the thumb and forefinger communicating to my intellect whether the soundboard is properly worked out to correspond with the guitar maker's concept and the sound required of the instrument."

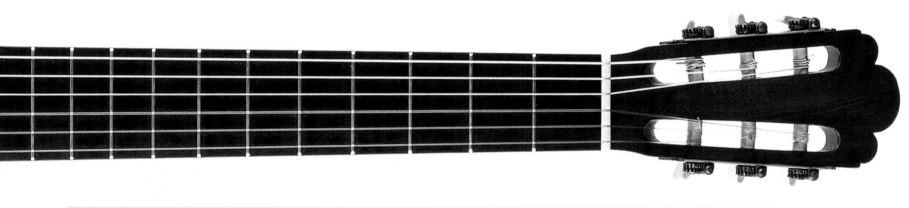

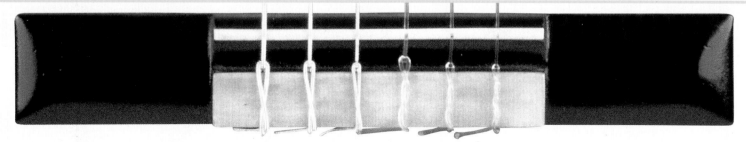

Above: *By Torres' time, pin-style bridges were being gradually replaced by this design, in which the strings pass through slots behind the saddle, and are tied into position.*

The Construction of Torres' Guitars

Torres' guitars were not radical departures from tradition, but reflections and refinements of many previous developments, molded into a masterful overall design that has provided a model for nearly all subsequent luthiers. Compared with earlier nineteenth-century French instruments (like those on pages 32-33), his bodies were larger and deeper, with a longer vibrating length for the strings (65cm/25.6in – now the standard for classical guitars) and a broader fingerboard. These changes, combined with Torres' improvements to the tops of his guitars, resulted in richer-sounding, more powerful instruments capable of responding to the technical and artistic needs of virtuoso performers. Torres was less concerned with decoration than his French and Spanish predecessors; his guitars are free from embellishments and elaborate inlays, and their elegant, understated appearance has set the tone for later instruments.

His advances in construction and bracing are based on the work of earlier Spanish luthiers, including Francisco Sanguino, Juan Pagés, and José Benedid. Their use of "fan-strutting" to reinforce the structure of the top (or plate) and modify the sound it produces contrasted with methods found elsewhere in Europe, where many makers preferred a system of transverse braces derived from lute design. This gave a bright, clear tone and a quick response when a note or chord was struck. Fan-strutting had a different effect, as British luthier Gary Southwell, who has built a number of Torres replicas, explains. "It's trying to control the plate a lot more, which tends to make the speaking time a bit slower, but gives you more harmonic richness of sound."

Torres' approach to fan-strutting, featuring seven braces (some previous makers had used as few as three), can be seen in the picture opposite, showing the underside of a Torres-style top built by Gary Southwell, and photographed before being glued into place. It provides a glimpse of Torres' solution to the perennial problem of making an instrument that is both tonally responsive and able to withstand the considerable pressure of its strings.

Right: Underside of top for a Torres replica guitar, made by Gary Southwell. The seven fan-struts reinforcing the lower part of the table are tapered, by careful planing, to the point where they meet the diagonal braces at its base. Two horizontal "harmonic bars" and two vertical supports strengthen the area around the soundhole. (COURTESY GARY SOUTHWELL)

Right: "Tornavoz" fitted to a guitar made by Francisco Simplicio, 1929. This device, thought to have been invented by Torres, is a brass or steel cylinder attached to the guitar's soundhole, and is intended to improve its projection. It was used by Torres on several of his instruments, and taken up by his later disciples, including Simplicio (1874–1932). The tornavoz is one of the few Torres innovations that failed to catch on more widely, but it may have influenced the development of other internally fitted units designed to boost the volume of steel-strung guitars. (COURTESY GARY SOUTHWELL)

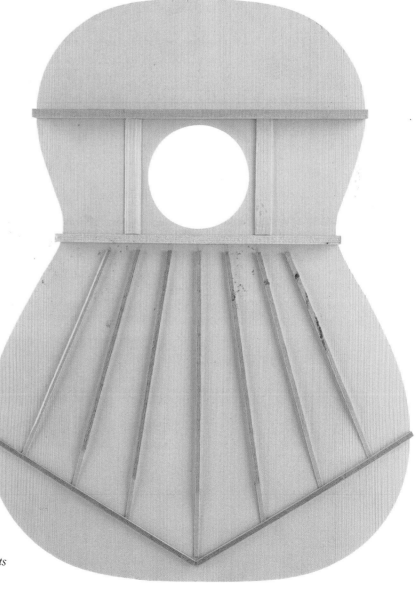

Tárrega and the Post-Torres Guitar

Francisco Tárrega (1852–1909) has been described as "the Chopin of the guitar" – a comparison that reflects his genius as one of its foremost players and composers. He was the first performer to demonstrate the increased tonal capabilities of the Torres-style instrument, and his extensive concert tours helped to spread its popularity throughout Europe. Tárrega was also an important teacher: his pupils included Emilio Pujol (1886–1980), Miguel Llobet (1878–1938), and a number of other players who later became highly influential in their own right.

As a young man, Tárrega met Torres during a visit to Seville in 1869, acquiring a guitar by the great luthier that he used almost exclusively for more than 20 years. During this period, he evolved a more expressive right-hand technique to make fuller use of the instrument's resources – although,

Above: Francisco Tárrega was born in Villareal in 1852, and died in Barcelona in 1909. He was the most distinguished guitarist of his generation, and also an accomplished composer, arranger, and pianist.

like many of his predecessors, he continued to strike the strings with his fingertips, not his nails. He also introduced a new playing position, in which the guitar was supported on the left thigh. (This improves balance, allowing the left and right hand to move more freely; earlier, smaller instruments had been perched on the performer's right thigh, on the edge of a chair, or even on a tripod.)

Although Tárrega never published a guitar tutor (his pupil and biographer Pujol issued a detailed account of his master's playing methods in the 1930s), he produced a considerable amount of music for the instrument. Many of his own pieces (notably the famous tremolo study *Recuerdos de la Alhambra*) have become staples of the classical repertoire, while his transcriptions of other composers' material helped to broaden the guitar's hitherto limited expressive range. They include effective arrangements of piano music by his contemporaries Enrique Granados (1867–1916) and Isaac Albéniz (1860–1909) – richly-textured, colorful compositions that would have been impossible to perform adequately on a pre-Torres guitar. Tárrega's achievements also caught the attention of younger composers, such as Manuel de Falla (1876–1946) and Heitor Villa-Lobos (1887–1959), who were later to write major works for the instrument.

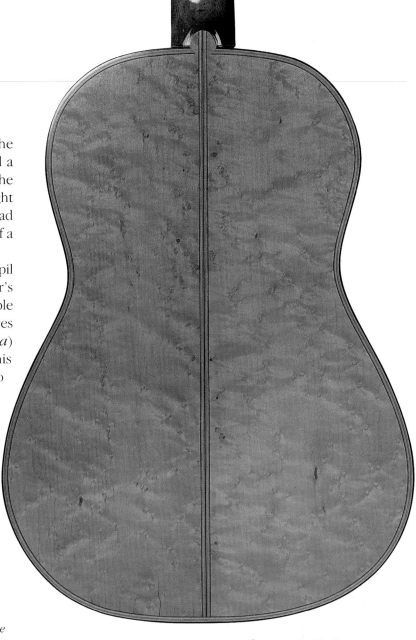

Left and above: *Guitar by Torres, 1889. The instrument's table is made from spruce, and has a finely decorated rosette; the rosewood bridge features bone edgings and mother-of-pearl dots. The back and sides of the guitar are bird's-eye maple; the fingerboard is ebony.* (COURTESY SHEL URLIK)

Left and right: *The label gives the instrument's date and number. Torres uses the words "segunda época" to differentiate his later (post-1875) guitars from those he made before his departure from Seville in 1869. The headstock is made from cypress; its face has a rosewood veneer.*

(COURTESY SHEL URLIK)

Towards the New World

By the mid-1800s, the guitar was growing in popularity not only in Europe, but also in the USA. It was first brought to the New World by the Spanish Conquistadores during the 1500s, and subsequently introduced to the native population in the schools set up by Franciscan monks throughout Spanish America. An English traveler, Thomas Gage, wrote of Indian children dancing "after the Spanish fashion to the sound of the guitarra" during his visit to a settlement near Mexico City in about 1625. Over the next hundred years, the instrument became increasingly popular with more privileged members of North American society. Guitars and printed tutors were readily available in many cities, and Benjamin Franklin (1706–1790) is said to have been a keen player.

Other plucked instruments came to America with its slaves. Among them were the banjo and the three-string "rabouquin," the close relative of an African instrument, the "raboukin," described by an eighteenth-century French

These pages: Christian Friedrich Martin made this guitar shortly before his departure from Germany to the United States. Its distinctive headstock follows the design created by Johann Georg Stauffer, the Viennese luthier for whom Martin worked in the 1820s.

(COURTESY EDINBURGH UNIVERSITY)

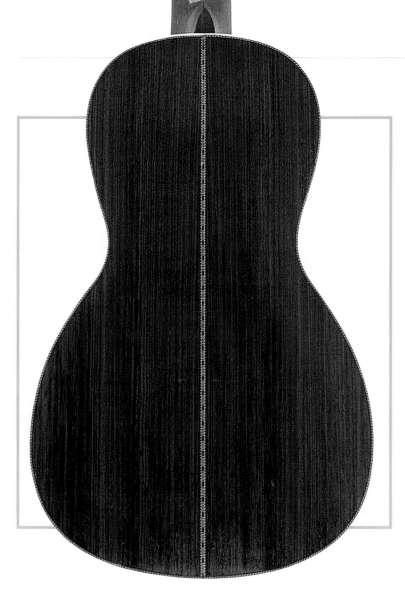

émigrés from Europe, bringing their skills and business acumen to their new home. They included Orville Gibson (1856–1918), who was born near New York of English parents, and later moved to Kalamazoo, Michigan, working as a clerk before devoting himself to instrument building in the 1880s. Orville's use of carved, arched tops on his mandolins and steel-strung guitars (an idea inspired by his study of violin design) was a key breakthrough in construction. It led to the formation of the Gibson Mandolin-Guitar Manufacturing Company in 1902, and eventually to the creation of Gibson's innovative archtop guitars of the 1920s and 1930s.

Significantly, another classic twentieth-century American archtop guitar firm, Epiphone, also had its roots in violin-making. The company was founded in New York in 1873 by a Greek instrument builder, Anastasios Stathopoulo. Originally known as the House of Stathopoulo, its new name came from Anastasios' son, Epaminondas (Epi), who took control of the business in the 1920s.

But the first, and arguably the most influential of all the Europeans who made acoustic guitars in America was C.F. Martin (1796–1873), a German luthier trained in Vienna, who settled in New York in 1833. The early history of his company is outlined on the next two pages.

explorer, François Le Vaillant, as a "triangular piece of board with three strings made of intestines…which may be stretched at pleasure by means of pegs, like those of our instruments in Europe." Many African-Americans also experimented with other, home-made instruments, including rough-and-ready guitars. But black players were, for obvious reasons, almost totally cut off from the developments in commercial guitar making that began to take place in the early decades of the nineteenth century.

Quite a number of the creators of the modern American guitar industry were first- or second-generation

C.F. Martin – Founding a Tradition

Christian Friedrich Martin was born in Mark Neukirchen, Saxony, on January 31, 1796. He took an early interest in woodworking, and learned the basics of the craft from his father, who was a cabinet maker. Soon, he was experimenting with building musical instruments, but after failing to gain an apprenticeship in his home town, he moved to Vienna in the 1820s, and was taken on by one of the leading guitar makers, Johann Georg Stauffer (1778–1853).

Martin eventually became the foreman at Stauffer's workshop, and was in day-to-day charge of the company's operations. However, he was keen to set up his own business, and left Vienna in 1825, returning to Saxony to try to fulfil his ambition. His plans were thwarted by the German violinmakers' guild, many of whom also built and sold guitars. They had a low opinion of guitar-makers, and did everything they could to prevent them from marketing their instruments. Martin fought and won a series of legal battles with the violinmakers' guild, but the lawsuits made life in Mark Neukirchen uncomfortable for him, and in 1833 he and his family emigrated to America.

Only a few months after arriving in New York, Martin opened a music shop at 196 Hudson Street, and for the next six years he built and sold his guitars from these premises. In 1839, he moved to eastern Pennsylvania, an area with a sizeable

German-speaking community. The Martin Company has been there ever since, and its acoustic guitars, made in Nazareth, Pennsylvania, have achieved world-wide fame. It has remained a family business: C.F. Martin's son, Christian Friedrich Jr., became head of the company after his father's death in 1873; and the current Chairman, Chris Martin IV, is the original C.F. Martin's great-great-great-grandson.

Above: Stauffer developed a mechanism allowing the angle of the neck to be manually adjusted – the key at the base of the neck controls this.

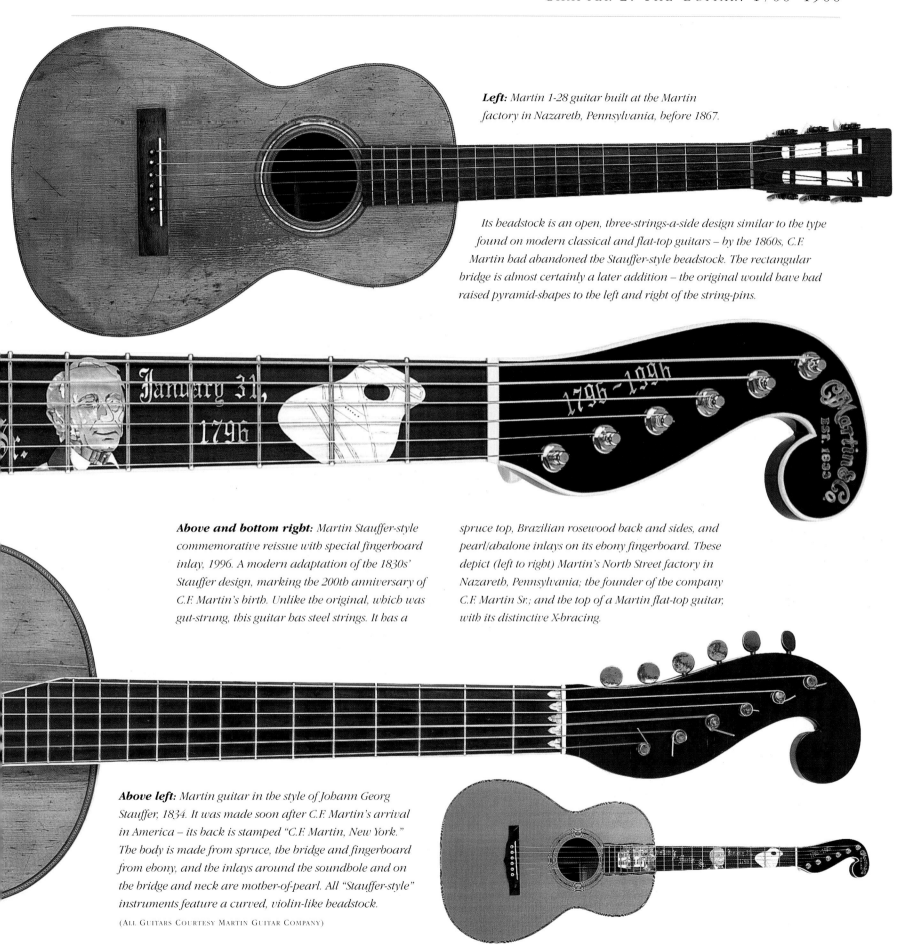

Left: *Martin 1-28 guitar built at the Martin factory in Nazareth, Pennsylvania, before 1867.*

Its headstock is an open, three-strings-a-side design similar to the type found on modern classical and flat-top guitars – by the 1860s, C.F. Martin had abandoned the Stauffer-style headstock. The rectangular bridge is almost certainly a later addition – the original would have had raised pyramid-shapes to the left and right of the string-pins.

Above and bottom right: *Martin Stauffer-style commemorative reissue with special fingerboard inlay, 1996. A modern adaptation of the 1830s' Stauffer design, marking the 200th anniversary of C.F. Martin's birth. Unlike the original, which was gut-strung, this guitar has steel strings. It has a* spruce top, Brazilian rosewood back and sides, and pearl/abalone inlays on its ebony fingerboard. These depict (left to right) Martin's North Street factory in Nazareth, Pennsylvania; the founder of the company C.F. Martin Sr.; and the top of a Martin flat-top guitar, with its distinctive X-bracing.

Above left: *Martin guitar in the style of Johann Georg Stauffer, 1834. It was made soon after C.F. Martin's arrival in America – its back is stamped "C.F. Martin, New York." The body is made from spruce, the bridge and fingerboard from ebony, and the inlays around the soundhole and on the bridge and neck are mother-of-pearl. All "Stauffer-style" instruments feature a curved, violin-like headstock.*

(ALL GUITARS COURTESY MARTIN GUITAR COMPANY)

49

SECTION TWO
Twentieth-Century Developments

By the early 1900s, the guitar had been slowly evolving for more than 300 years – but the pace of change was soon to change dramatically, with a range of radical innovations, driven by the demands of the American market, quickly bringing the instrument to the forefront of popular music. Accordingly, this section focuses on the USA and examines the work of the individuals and companies who helped to fashion the modern acoustic guitar.

At the turn of the century, guitars were still outsold by banjos and mandolins, which dominated solo and group playing. By contrast, the guitar's place was mainly in the home – as an instrument to play in the parlor with family and friends, and as an accompaniment for singing. The main cause of this musical limitation was lack of volume, and as early as the 1880s, a number of makers were experimenting with the use of louder, more durable steel strings instead of the traditional gut sets. Their sound was not to everyone's liking. *Winner's Practical School for the Guitar*, an instruction book published in 1884, castigated the "cranks [who] choose steel strings, which are an abomination; any piece of pine board will answer just as well for an instrument to such depraved tastes". Nevertheless, the demand for them was strong, and by the mid-1930s, archtop, flat-top and resonator guitars, all steel-strung, were firmly established in American (and increasingly in European) popular music. The next chapters look in detail at their design and development, and show how these instruments have continued to evolve in the last half-century.

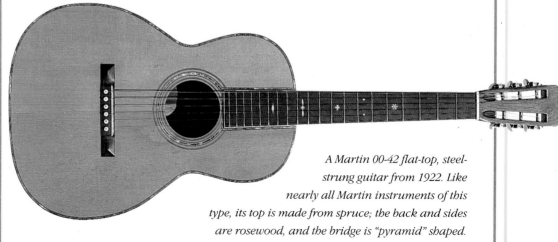

A Martin 00-42 flat-top, steel-strung guitar from 1922. Like nearly all Martin instruments of this type, its top is made from spruce; the back and sides are rosewood, and the bridge is "pyramid" shaped.

(COURTESY REAL GUITARS, SAN FRANCISCO)

CHAPTER 3
TOWARDS THE MODERN GUITAR

Orville Gibson (1856–1918) was the first major American luthier to apply the techniques of European violin-making to fretted instruments. During his childhood in Chateaugay, a small town in northern New York state, he had developed considerable skills as a wood-carver, as well as a strong interest in music. Later, he moved west to Kalamazoo, Michigan, where he began his professional instrument-building career in the early 1890s.

Orville's early efforts included a number of violins – one of them made out of wood salvaged from the old Town Hall in Boston – and he went on to introduce violin-like, arched soundboards to his ground-breaking mandolin designs; previously, the instrument had always been fitted with a flat or bent top. He later developed and patented another innovative design idea: the construction of a mandolin's neck and sides from the same piece of wood, with a partial hollowing-out of its neck to increase the instrument's internal volume.

Orville Gibson's guitars displayed many of the same characteristics as his mandolins, with carved, arched tops, and oval "Neapolitan"-style soundholes. During construction, their fronts and backs were "tuned" (to optimize their resonating properties) by a painstaking process of tapping and carving identical to the methods used by European violin-builders. The guitars, which were fitted with steel strings as standard, were also considerably larger than any other contemporary luthier's; Gibson's biggest six-string model was 18 inches (45.7cm) wide. These features – combined with their elegant, often elaborately decorated appearance – made "Orville-style" instruments unique, and ensured their popularity among players looking for powerful, richer-sounding guitars.

The success of Orville's mandolin and guitar designs led to the formation of the Gibson Mandolin-Guitar Manufacturing Company in 1902. Surprisingly, he was only a consultant to the business, not its owner, and his direct involvement with it was relatively brief. He left Kalamazoo in 1909, and died in 1918, a year before the firm recruited Lloyd Loar – the brilliant young designer who was to take the archtop mandolin and guitar to new levels of sophistication and excellence.

Below left: *Gibson Style O, early 1900s. This model was introduced in 1902; the distinctive crescent and star inlay on the headstock was used on several of the first Gibsons. Unlike most other guitar makers of the period, Gibson fitted its instruments with steel strings as standard.*
(COURTESY ELDERLY INSTRUMENTS; PHOTOGRAPH BY DAVE MATCHETTE)

The Gibson Style O later underwent considerable changes; a new version, launched in 1908, featured a scrolled body design, an elevated pickguard, and a floating bridge with a metal tailpiece. The model was eventually discontinued in 1923.

Left: *Gibson Style U harp guitar, c.1915. Harp guitars were designed to provide players with an extended bass range, which was particularly useful for ensemble work. On this model, the ten "extra" strings would probably have been tuned chromatically.*
(COURTESY ELDERLY INSTRUMENTS; PHOTOGRAPH BY DAVE MATCHETTE)

Martin and the Birth of the American Flat-top

The Martin Company was already well-established by the time Orville Gibson began his career, and its guitar designs had evolved along very different lines. C. F. Martin Sr. (1796–1873) never used carved soundboards; he built his instruments with traditional flat tops, and, as we have seen, his earliest guitars were strongly influenced by the work of his former employer, the Viennese luthier Johann Georg Stauffer. However, soon after Martin's move from New York to Pennsylvania in 1839, one distinctive "Stauffer-style" feature, the scrolled headstock with its six-a-side tuning machines, began to be phased out in favor of a rectangular head like the one seen on the instruments below. The company's current Chairman, Chris Martin IV, suggests that the reason for this was, in fact, purely practical: "The story I heard was that the tuning machine mechanism came from Europe, probably Germany…and the supply would occasionally be disrupted. So he would have guitars all ready to go, and no tuning machines. That's why he went to the rectangular headstock."

Another important innovation took place in the 1850s, when the Martin Company introduced a system of X-bracing on the insides of its guitar soundboards. (Previous Martin guitars had been fitted with a form of lateral strutting.) C.F. Martin may well have invented this revolutionary design, and was certainly responsible for developing and popularizing it, and X-bracing later became a major factor in the success and longevity of Martin's classic twentieth-century steel-strung designs.

Steel strings were not fitted as standard on Martin guitars until 1922, although they were available as an option on some models from 1900 onwards. But many other now-familiar aspects of the Martin range were firmly in place well before the turn of the century. The system of identifying models by two hyphenated codes – the first denoting body size, the second "style" and materials – was adopted in the 1850s, and is still in use today. One of those designated "styles," Style 18, has been in regular production for over 140 years, and a number of other current models are also closely based on C.F. Martin Sr.'s original flat-top designs.

Left: *Martin 000-42, 1918. The 000 size, which has a body width of 15 inches (38.1cm), was introduced in 1902 in response to players' demands for larger, louder guitars. This Style 42 is strung with steel, and has a distinctive ivory bridge.*
(COURTESY ERIC SCHOENBERG)

Right: *An early example of a gut-strung Martin Style 18 guitar, from about 1870. The style was first introduced in 1857, and is still being made. This model is a "size 2 ½", with a body width of 11⅝in (29.5cm).*
(COURTESY ERIC SCHOENBERG)

Above: *A rare Martin 000-21 harp-guitar, built in 1902. Unlike the Gibson Style "U" shown earlier, this instrument has two necks; the upper one is an unfretted support for the extra 12 strings. These would have been used as "drones," or to provide extra bass notes.* (COURTESY MARTIN GUITAR COMPANY)

Gibson – the "L" Range

After the launch of the Gibson Mandolin-Guitar Manufacturing Company in 1902, the mainstay of the company's guitar range was the "L" series. There were initially four "L" models listed, but the original "Style L" was soon dropped from the catalog, the L-2 was discontinued in 1908, and the L-1 and L-3 were joined in 1911 by the larger L-4.

The instruments retained the steel strings and arched tops introduced by Orville Gibson, but differed substantially from his previous designs in other ways. They were plainer than their predecessors; Orville's love of elaborately inlaid soundboards, fingerboards, and bridges was probably not commercially sustainable, and Gibson designs became increasingly standardized after his departure from Kalamazoo in 1909. The early "L" series guitars were smaller than the "Orville-style" instruments – the L-1 and L-3 had a body width of 13½ inches (34.3cm), and the biggest model in the series, the L-4, was a modest 16 inches (40.6cm) wide. And the "L" series also abandoned some of Orville's ingenious ideas about internal construction, including his method of building an instrument's sides and neck from a single piece of wood.

However, by the end of World War I, other important new construction techniques were under development at Gibson. A member of the workforce,

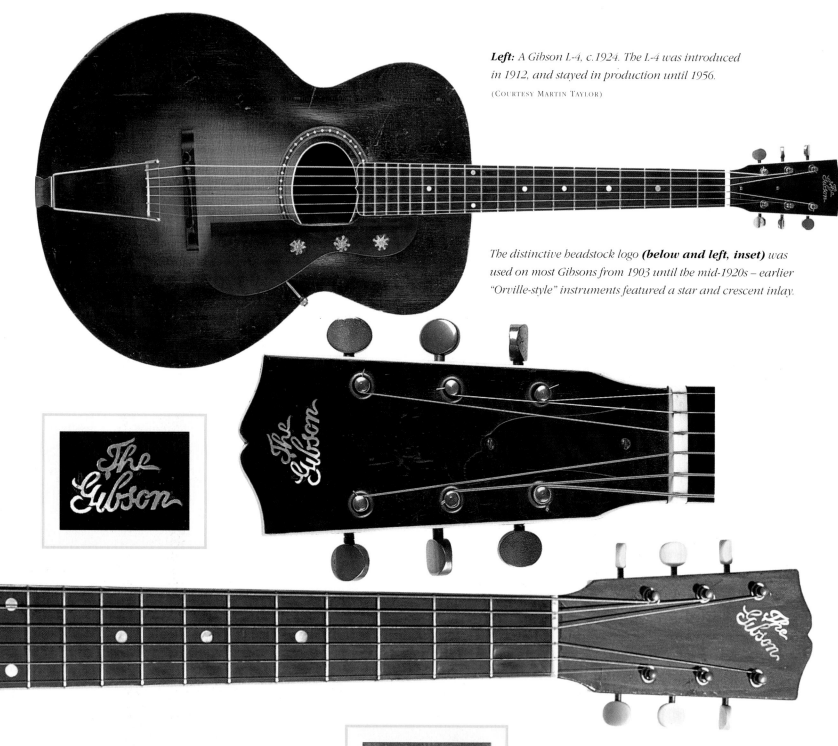

Left: A Gibson L-4, c.1924. The L-4 was introduced in 1912, and stayed in production until 1956. (COURTESY MARTIN TAYLOR)

The distinctive headstock logo **(below and left, inset)** *was used on most Gibsons from 1903 until the mid-1920s – earlier "Orville-style" instruments featured a star and crescent inlay.*

Ted McHugh, was responsible for the introduction of the truss-rod – a steel bar, fitted inside the neck, which greatly improved the guitar's strength and rigidity, and allowed the neck itself to be made slimmer and more comfortable for the player. Truss-rods were fitted as standard to most Gibson guitars from 1922 onwards (Gibson quickly patented the concept); the triangular cover for the one on the L-4 above can be seen

Above left and left, inset: A Gibson L-1, c.1920. A late example of an archtop design first produced by Gibson in 1902. (COURTESY REAL GUITARS, SAN FRANCISCO)

clearly in the close-up picture. But the guitar that displayed the most dramatic design breakthroughs was the L-5, which set the standard for all subsequent archtop guitars, and was the brainchild of Gibson's chief instrument designer, Lloyd Loar.

CHAPTER 4
AMERICAN ARCHTOPS

*L*loyd Allayre Loar (1886–1943) possessed an unusual combination of talents. He was a music graduate and a skilled performer on the mandolin and viola, as well as an engineer with a keen grasp of the technical aspects of instrument design. During his five-year stay at Gibson, he was responsible for product development, improving existing models and experimenting with new concepts, including electric guitars. But his great contribution to the evolution of the acoustic instrument was his work on the Gibson L-5, which first appeared in 1922, and is now recognized as one of the most important and influential archtops ever built.

Like Orville Gibson, Loar made his first breakthroughs in mandolin design, and then applied these innovations to the construction of the guitar. In 1922, he introduced the Gibson F-5, a mandolin that took Orville's innovative arched-top construction one stage further by using f-holes in place of the instrument's customary oval sound-hole. Later that year, the L-5 guitar appeared; it, too, had f-holes, as well as a number of other new features: a truss-rod, an adjustable bridge, and a system of top bracing that used two parallel wooden bars glued to the inside of the soundboard. The result was a guitar with a winning combination of playability, tone-quality, and power, which was quickly taken up by a number of extremely influential American players – notably Eddie Lang (1902–1933), whose recordings with fellow-guitarist Lonnie Johnson (1889–1970), and collaborations with violinist Joe Venuti

(1903–1978) helped to establish the guitar as a solo instrument in jazz.

Gibson responded to the resultant demand by bringing out three other "L" series archtops; the first of these, the L-10, was officially launched in 1931. It bore a strong resemblance to the L-5, but was not designed by Lloyd Loar, who left the firm in 1924 after it refused to back his plans to produce electric instruments. He continued to develop his radical ideas until the war years, setting up his own company, Vivi-Tone, with two other ex-Gibson employees in 1933.

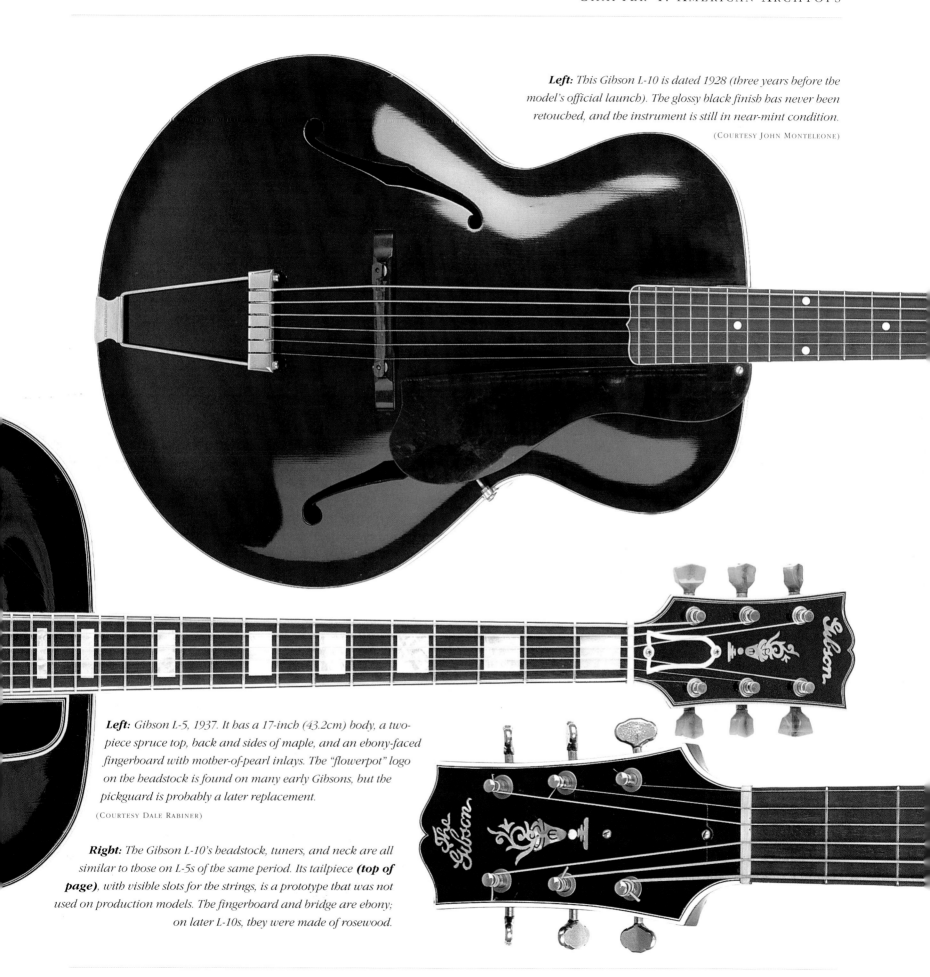

Left: *This Gibson L-10 is dated 1928 (three years before the model's official launch). The glossy black finish has never been retouched, and the instrument is still in near-mint condition.*

(COURTESY JOHN MONTELEONE)

Left: *Gibson L-5, 1937. It has a 17-inch (43.2cm) body, a two-piece spruce top, back and sides of maple, and an ebony-faced fingerboard with mother-of-pearl inlays. The "flowerpot" logo on the headstock is found on many early Gibsons, but the pickguard is probably a later replacement.*

(COURTESY DALE RABINER)

Right: *The Gibson L-10's headstock, tuners, and neck are all similar to those on L-5s of the same period. Its tailpiece (top of page), with visible slots for the strings, is a prototype that was not used on production models. The fingerboard and bridge are ebony; on later L-10s, they were made of rosewood.*

Gibson – from L-5 to Super 400

ibson continued to refine and develop its range of archtop guitars throughout the 1930s. The L-5 remained a key instrument in this range, but Lloyd Loar's original design underwent a number of changes in the years following his departure. In 1934, Gibson addressed the perennial need for extra power and volume by increasing the body width of the L-5 from 16 inches to 17 inches (40.6 to 43.2cm). At the same time, it enlarged three other "L" models (the L-10, L-7, and L-12) by the same amount, and introduced a new, top-of-the-line archtop with an 18-inch (45.7cm) body, the Super 400.

This guitar was designed to impress – a lavishly decorated flagship for the Gibson range, taking its name from its $400 price tag (a substantial sum, especially in the Depression years). It featured gold-plated tuning machines, pearl inlays, an ebony fingerboard, and an elaborate tailpiece with the model's name engraved on it. The Super 400 was highly acclaimed – among the players who could afford it – and it remains in use today, although some guitarists find it too large for comfort, and question whether its sound is significantly more powerful than a 17-inch Gibson's.

Gibson was the early pioneer of archtop guitar design, but by the mid-1930s it was no longer alone in the market. Epiphone had introduced a rival range of instruments in 1931, and several other important guitar-makers (including Stromberg and D'Angelico, whose work will be examined later in this chapter) were also launching new instruments. Gibson had to innovate to survive; and the company's next major development, the cutaway body, was introduced as an option on the L-5 and the Super 400 in 1939 (see photograph opposite). Cutaways gave the player easier access to the higher reaches of the fingerboard; they

were an immediate success, and not surprisingly, they were soon adopted by Gibson's competitors.

Despite such rivalry, and the growing demand for electric guitars in the post-war years, the L-5 and Super 400 acoustics retained their place in the main Gibson catalog until the 1980s, and are still available as part of the company's "Historic Collection" series.

Right: *Gibson L-7, 1937. The L-7 first appeared in 1932, and was enlarged from 16 inches to 17 inches (40.6 to 43.2cm) in 1934.*

Left: Gibson L-12P, 1948. The L-12 was introduced a year after the L-7; the "P" (standing for Premier) designates a cutaway model. The "crown" inlay on the headstock and the parallelogram fingerboard decoration **(opposite page, inset)** are still seen on many Gibson guitars today.

(COURTESY MANDOLIN BROTHERS, NEW YORK)

Right: The Gibson L7 features delicate mother-of-pearl "picture-frame" inlays on its fingerboard.

(COURTESY MANDOLIN BROTHERS, NEW YORK)

Left: This is a modern replica, from Gibson's "Historic Collection," of a 1939-style Super 400.

(COURTESY DALE RABINER)

Epiphone – A Rival Range of Archtops

Epaminondas ("Epi") Stathopoulo (1893–1943) became President of his father Anastasios' New York-based instrument building company, the House of Stathopoulo, in the 1920s. For a number of years, the company had concentrated on banjo-making, and it was renamed the Epiphone Banjo Corporation in 1928. But in the early 1930s, Epiphone changed direction, focusing on the design and production of guitars, and providing the market-leaders, Gibson, with some serious competition.

Epiphone constantly sought to outdo Gibson's innovations. It challenged the dominant position of the L-5 with the launch of its "Masterbilt" range, comprising no fewer than nine new archtops, in 1931. When Gibson increased the body sizes on its guitars, Epiphone made its products a little larger still. And the company's two highly-acclaimed flagship guitars, the De Luxe (1931) and the Emperor (1936), were conceived as direct rivals to their Gibson counterparts, the L-5 and the Super 400.

But Epiphone was certainly not a mere imitator. Its guitars were the fruit of many years' experience in stringed-instrument construction, and were immediately recognizable onstage, with their asymmetrical headstocks and elegant pearl inlays. The "wandering vine" design shown opposite was seen on most Epiphones from the 1930s to the 1950s, and the company also used distinctive floral, diamond, and cloud-shaped markers for its fingerboards. Another Epiphone feature was the "Frequensator" tailpiece (seen on the Emperor and 1959 Deluxe models); it was intended to "equalize" treble and bass response by shortening the top three strings' path from bridge to tailpiece, and extending the length of the lower strings. It is doubtful whether this made much difference to the sound, but the simple elegance of the "double trapeze" design ensured its lasting popularity.

Above: *Epiphone's distinctive "epsilon" logo on the pickguard of the 1959 Deluxe.*

Epiphone's post-war history has been a checkered one. Epi Stathopoulo died in 1943, and ten years later his family sold the business. Ironically, it eventually ended up in the hands of Chicago Musical Instruments (CMI), which also owned Gibson, and for a while Epiphones were made at their old competitor's Kalamazoo factory. Since the 1970s, guitars bearing the Epiphone label have been built in the Far East.

Left: *Epiphone De Luxe, 1935. This model features Epiphone's famous "wandering vine" design on its headstock, which has an off-center groove on its right-hand side – another "trademark" for early Epiphone instruments. The top is spruce, the back and sides maple.*

(COURTESY MARTIN TAYLOR)

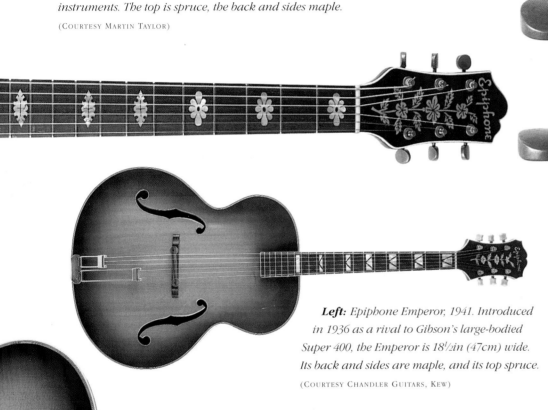

Left: *Epiphone Emperor, 1941. Introduced in 1936 as a rival to Gibson's large-bodied Super 400, the Emperor is 18½in (47cm) wide. Its back and sides are maple, and its top spruce.*

(COURTESY CHANDLER GUITARS, KEW)

Left and right: *This Deluxe dates from 1959, and has a cutaway and a "Frequensator" tailpiece. The pickup (a De Armond model popular with many archtop players) is attached to the neck and pickguard, and does not affect the instrument's acoustic sound.*

(COURTESY MANDOLIN BROTHERS, NEW YORK)

Stromberg and the "Orchestral" Archtop

Like Epiphone, Charles A. Stromberg & Son was a family firm. Its founder, Charles Stromberg, had emigrated from Sweden to Boston, Massachusetts; after working for a prominent local instrument manufacturer, Thompson and Odell, for a number of years, he formed his own company, which made drums and xylophones as well as banjos, mandolins, and guitars, in about 1905. Five years later, Charles' son, Elmer (1895–1955) joined the business as a 15-year-old trainee.

Elmer worked on a wide variety of instruments, and made his initial reputation in the 1920s as a banjo designer. During this period, he had also begun to build archtop guitars, producing them in larger numbers as the banjo began to decline in popularity. The earliest Stromberg archtops were the "G" series: they had 16-inch (40.6cm) bodies, and were introduced in the late 1920s.

Like many other luthiers, Elmer Stromberg followed Gibson in increasing the size of his guitars. His G-1, G-2, and Deluxe models were widened to 17 inches (43.2cm) in the mid-1930s, and in 1937 he added two new instruments to the range: the Master 300 and 400. These were the largest and among the most powerful-sounding archtops available, with a body width of 19 inches (48.3cm), and they proved popular with big-band players; Stromberg's customers included Count Basie's guitarist, Freddie Green, Frank Bittles of the Fletcher Henderson Orchestra, and Fred Guy from Duke Ellington's band.

Elmer Stromberg constantly developed and modified his designs. One of his most important innovations was a new system of top bracing, replacing the parallel wooden struts he had used on his early guitars with a single diagonal bar running across the inside of his instruments' soundboards. This was in use on all his guitars by 1940, and was followed by other refinements, including truss-rod systems and (after the war) body cutaways. The general trend towards electric archtops in the 1950s did not reduce the demand for Strombergs, and the production of instruments was only halted by Elmer's untimely death in 1955.

Left: This Stromberg Deluxe cutaway dates from the early 1950s. It is slightly smaller than the Master 400 (just over 17 inches, 48.3cm wide) but retains the distinctive headstock and tailpiece design.

(COURTESY MANDOLIN BROTHERS, NEW YORK)

Below and right: *Stromberg Master 400, 1948, made for Frank Bittles, guitarist with Fletcher Henderson. It has a spruce top, back and sides of maple, and an ebony strip inset into its maple neck.*

(COURTESY DERRICK WESKIN)

*The body of the Stromberg Master 400 **(left)** is 19 inches (48.3cm) wide. Its headstock decoration **(bottom of page)** is not a pearl inlay, but has been carved out of the layers of plastic covering the wood.*

D'Angelico –
A New York Classic

Archtop guitars by John D'Angelico (1905–1964) are among the finest instruments of their kind. Born into an Italian-American family in New York, D'Angelico was steeped in the traditions of European instrument building, and at the age of nine he began learning the basics of his craft from his great-uncle, who was a distinguished maker of Italian-style mandolins and violins. In 1932, D'Angelico set up his own workshop at 40 Kenmare Street, New York City, and started to develop his own guitar designs, which were strongly influenced by the Gibson L-5. Even at this early stage in his career, he was already attracting commissions from leading players. The "No. 2" instrument shown opposite was made for Benny Martell, the guitarist with the Buddy Rogers Orchestra – which had the dubious distinction of being a particular favorite of the American gangster Al Capone!

By 1937, D'Angelico was offering his customers four models of archtop guitar: Style A, Style B, the Excel, and the New Yorker. The first two designs were phased out during the early 1940s, and the Excel and New Yorker are the instruments on which his reputation rests. The Excel has a 17-inch

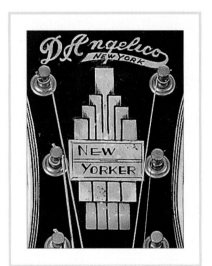

(43.2cm) body, and its distinctive cut-out headstock and urn-shaped "finial" were soon used on the larger-sized New Yorker as well. Both models underwent considerable changes over the years; D'Angelico would often add custom features tailored to his customers' requirements, as well as replacing or upgrading parts of his guitars when they were returned to his workshop for maintenance or adjustments.

Despite the substantial demand for his instruments, D'Angelico rarely made more than 30 guitars a year. They were built by hand with the help of two assistants – the first of whom, Jimmy DiSerio, left the firm in 1959. For the last five years of his life, D'Angelico's only regular employee was his apprentice Jimmy D'Aquisto, who had started work with him in 1951, and came to play an increasingly important role as D'Angelico's health deteriorated and he suffered a series of heart attacks. Most of the instruments produced during this final period were built by D'Aquisto under his master's guidance. Following D'Angelico's death, D'Aquisto quickly established himself as a distinguished luthier in his own right.

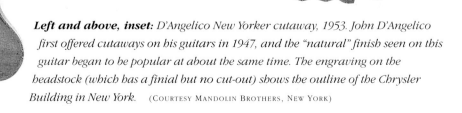

Right and opposite page, inset: D'Angelico No. 2, 1932. This guitar, previously owned by Benny Martell of the Buddy Rogers Orchestra, has been restored by luthier John Monteleone. Like most D'Angelicos, it is made from American woods: the top is sitka spruce, the back and sides red maple. The pickguard is a later addition, probably made by John D'Angelico himself. (COURTESY JOHN MONTELEONE)

Left and above, inset: D'Angelico New Yorker cutaway, 1953. John D'Angelico first offered cutaways on his guitars in 1947, and the "natural" finish seen on this guitar began to be popular at about the same time. The engraving on the headstock (which has a finial but no cut-out) shows the outline of the Chrysler Building in New York. (COURTESY MANDOLIN BROTHERS, NEW YORK)

Right: *D'Angelico Excel, 1939, with a 17-inch (43.2cm) body, pearl fingerboard inlays engraved with a distinctive diagonal pattern, and D'Angelico's "trademark" headstock, with its "keyhole" cut-out and finial.*
(COURTESY MANDOLIN BROTHERS, NEW YORK)

D'Aquisto –
From Pupil to Master

Jimmy D'Aquisto (1935–1995) had been very close to John D'Angelico, and after the death of his former employer and mentor in 1964, he continued making D'Angelico's classic archtop guitar designs, the Excel and the New Yorker, under his own name. As D'Aquisto's friend and fellow-luthier John Monteleone explains, "Jimmy was bound by tradition. He had such a reverence for John [D'Angelico] that it took him a long time to build himself up to trusting himself. He had to prove himself to the people who loved John's work and solicited John's shop, and he did it by making his guitars just like John's – or as much as he could. Jimmy was always torn between living the legacy of John and being himself."

Gradually, D'Aquisto began to invest D'Angelico's designs with variations of his own. He altered the appearance of the f-holes on his Excels and New Yorkers, making them into elliptical s-shapes, and began using adjustable tailpieces with an ebony top and a brass hinge. On some models (see photograph opposite) he dispensed with D'Angelico's trademark finial, and streamlined the appearance of the pickguard. John Monteleone describes the motivation behind these and other changes as the desire to break away from tradition, "to carry the instruments on from where they've left off," and this process continued with D'Aquisto's later guitars, which are strikingly original and effective re-interpretations of the "traditional" archtop.

Perhaps the most radical example of D'Aquisto's design philosophy is his "Solo" model – an instrument fittingly summarized by John Monteleone as "playable art." It has a carved-out headstock, dramatically reshaped soundholes intended to in-crease the guitar's projection, and a body made from spruce and Tyrolean maple (Euro-pean "cello-wood"– D'Aquisto rarely used American woods for his acoustics). He made only nine Solos before his sudden death in April 1995, and among the advance orders he left unful-filled was one from composer and guitarist Craig Snyder, who subsequently asked John Monteleone if he would be prepared to make a version of the Solo for him. The remarkable outcome of this request can be seen overleaf.

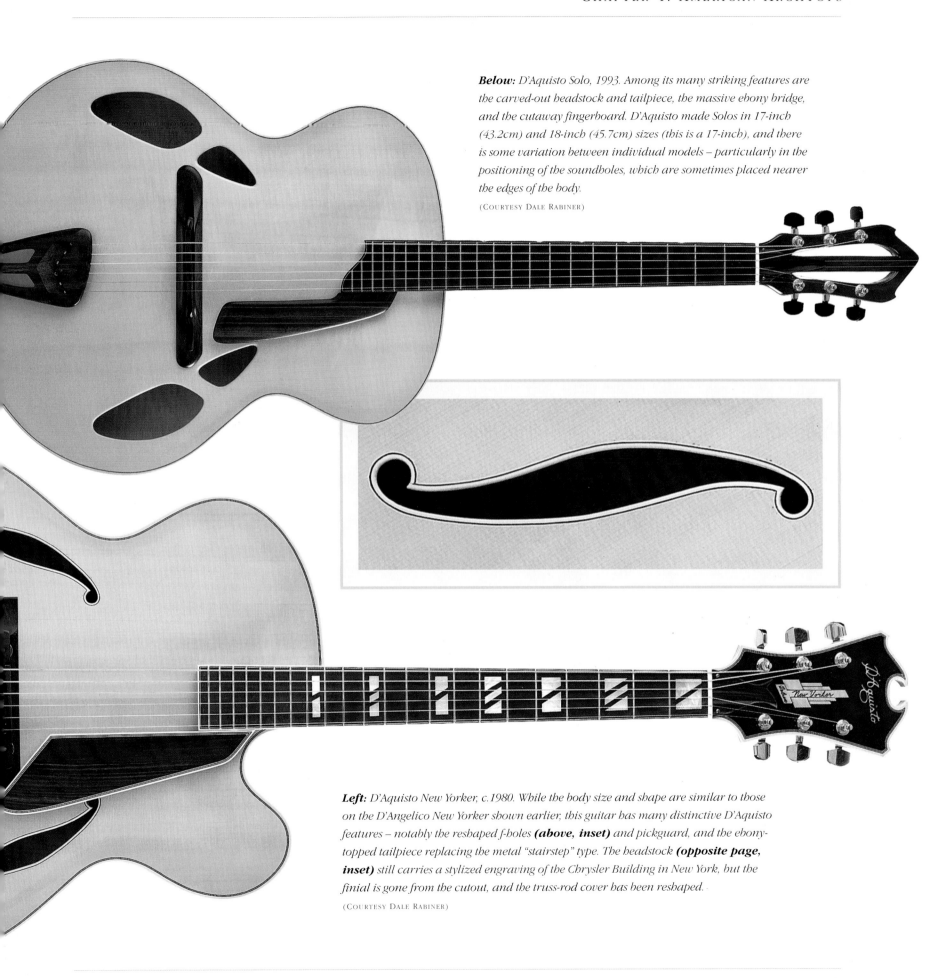

Below: *D'Aquisto Solo, 1993. Among its many striking features are the carved-out headstock and tailpiece, the massive ebony bridge, and the cutaway fingerboard. D'Aquisto made Solos in 17-inch (43.2cm) and 18-inch (45.7cm) sizes (this is a 17-inch), and there is some variation between individual models – particularly in the positioning of the soundholes, which are sometimes placed nearer the edges of the body.*

(COURTESY DALE RABINER)

Left: *D'Aquisto New Yorker, c.1980. While the body size and shape are similar to those on the D'Angelico New Yorker shown earlier, this guitar has many distinctive D'Aquisto features – notably the reshaped f-holes* **(above, inset)** *and pickguard, and the ebony-topped tailpiece replacing the metal "stairstep" type. The headstock* **(opposite page, inset)** *still carries a stylized engraving of the Chrysler Building in New York, but the finial is gone from the cutout, and the truss-rod cover has been reshaped.*

(COURTESY DALE RABINER)

John Monteleone's "Montequisto"

When he was commissioned by Craig Snyder to build a "Solo" guitar based closely on Jimmy D'Aquisto's original design, John Monteleone selected materials from D'Aquisto's own workshop, including wood, lacquer, and a partially completed neck and set of sides. Monteleone also had access to a number of earlier D'Aquisto Solos, taking tracings from them and examining their construction carefully. He explains that "out of respect for Jimmy, I felt it was a good idea to stay as close to the original design as possible. I knew that I could never duplicate the sound, and that wasn't my intention. Someone's sound and their tone is their thumbprint – and realizing that, when I got to building the inside of the guitar, I knew that I'd have to rely on my own instincts and experience to get the best tone I could for this particular guitar. I stayed pretty close to the concept, but yet I went my own way a little bit, just to conduct it as I thought would be best." The outcome – a magnificent creation nicknamed the "Montequisto" by John's wife – is shown opposite.

Monteleone's own instruments (he builds flat-top guitars and mandolins as well as acoustic and electric archtops) are highly sought after by leading players. His close knowledge of the work of Jimmy D'Aquisto, John D'Angelico, and other leading luthiers, as well as his extensive experience as a guitar restorer, give him a special insight into the technical aspects of instrument construction. But he also draws inspiration from key figures in other areas of design – notably Raymond Loewy, who created the Lucky Strike cigarette packet, the Studebaker Avanti motorcar, and other classic American artifacts. Like Loewy and other commercial designers, Monteleone stresses the importance of simplicity and functionality in his work:

"I never have an individual element of the guitar compete against another one. The first requirement is that [the instrument] has to play up to expectations. Once you've achieved that, then you can begin to look at how to make the parts harmonious in their appearance. It's another kind of vibration. The guitar has a sound – but it also has a look that moves."

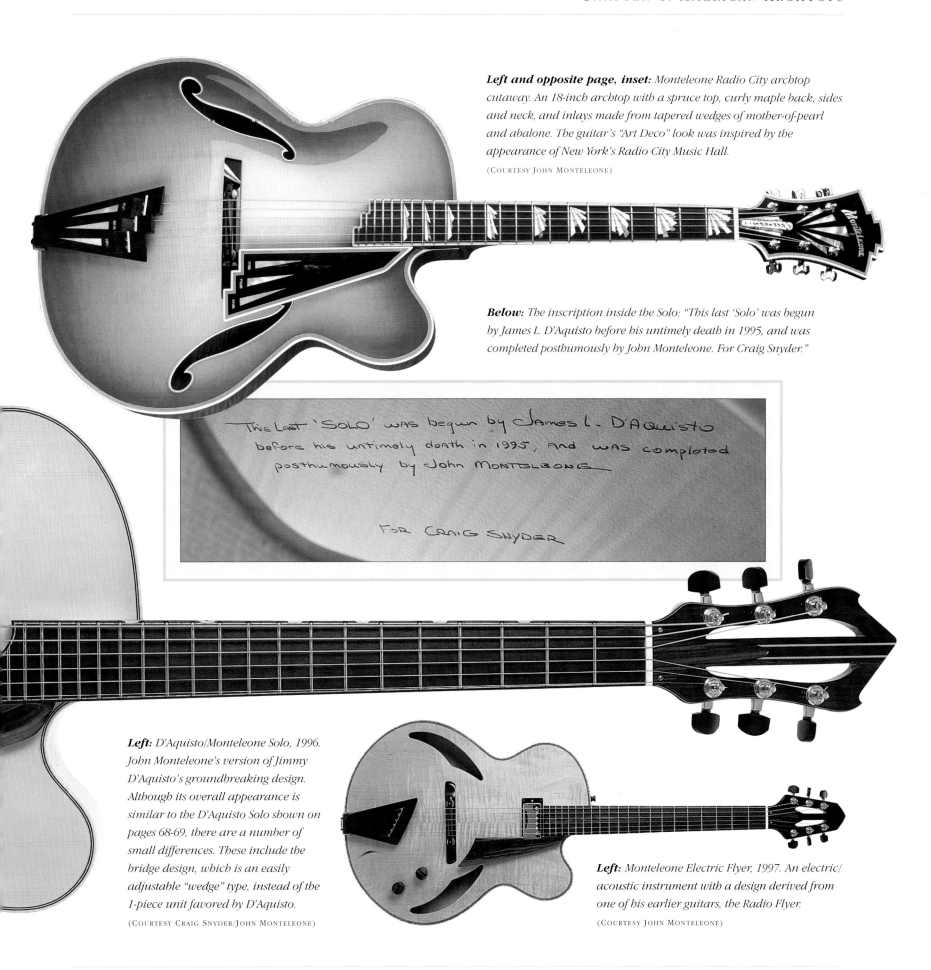

Left and opposite page, inset: *Monteleone Radio City archtop cutaway. An 18-inch archtop with a spruce top, curly maple back, sides and neck, and inlays made from tapered wedges of mother-of-pearl and abalone. The guitar's "Art Deco" look was inspired by the appearance of New York's Radio City Music Hall.*
(COURTESY JOHN MONTELEONE)

Below: *The inscription inside the Solo: "This last 'Solo' was begun by James L. D'Aquisto before his untimely death in 1995, and was completed posthumously by John Monteleone. For Craig Snyder."*

This Last 'SOLO' was begun by James L. D'Aquisto before his untimely death in 1995, And was completed posthumously by John MONTELEONE

FOR CRAIG SNYDER

Left: *D'Aquisto/Monteleone Solo, 1996. John Monteleone's version of Jimmy D'Aquisto's groundbreaking design. Although its overall appearance is similar to the D'Aquisto Solo shown on pages 68-69, there are a number of small differences. These include the bridge design, which is an easily adjustable "wedge" type, instead of the 1-piece unit favored by D'Aquisto.*
(COURTESY CRAIG SNYDER/JOHN MONTELEONE)

Left: *Monteleone Electric Flyer, 1997. An electric/acoustic instrument with a design derived from one of his earlier guitars, the Radio Flyer.*
(COURTESY JOHN MONTELEONE)

Robert Benedetto and "The Sound of Today"

Robert Benedetto was born in the Bronx, New York in 1946. His father and grandfather were master cabinet-makers (his grandfather worked for the Steinway Piano Company), and the skills he learned from them, combined with his passion for music, led to his first childhood experiments in creating instruments – miniature replicas that he carved out of discarded scraps of wood, using a knife he made from one of his grandfather's files. Bob soon graduated to building real guitars; and after a spell as a professional player, and service in the U.S. Air Force, he became a full-time archtop luthier in 1968. He now makes his world-famous instruments at his home in East Stroudsburg, Pennsylvania – with his grandfather's tools still close to hand.

Bob's designs have a strong affinity with European traditions of stringed instrument making; he produces violins, violas, and mandolins, as well as archtop guitars, and has recently completed his first cello. He acknowledges that "violin-makers have certainly been an inspiration to me – more so than guitar-makers really," and says he finds violins a greater challenge to build than guitars. "A violin is either 'right' or it's 'wrong' – there's very little room for subjectivity, and violin players are more in agreement than guitarists on what their instrument should play and feel and sound like."

Bob's approach to archtop guitar design is based on years of practical experience as a player and luthier. He uses X-braced tops, which provide the combination of warmth and well-balanced tone he describes as "the sound of today" for the soloist. He has also moved away from the large, heavy body construction favored by some earlier makers; Benedetto archtops are lighter and more responsive, with distinctively shaped tailpieces made from ebony – not the more massive brass seen on other instruments in this chapter. Bob comments that "big isn't necessarily better or louder," and says the most popular body size for his archtops is 17 inches (43.2cm) – although he also builds 16-inch (40.6cm) and 18-inch (45.7cm) guitars.

In his 30-year career, Benedetto has completed more than 675 instruments (over 400 are archtops), and is generally regarded as the leading archtop builder of his generation.

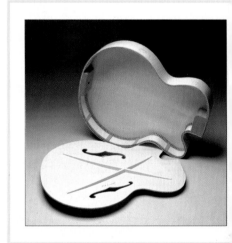

Below: *Benedetto La Venezia (18-inch left-hand model) in a shaded natural finish. The top is made from European spruce, the back from highly flamed European maple. There are no bindings or inlays. The fingerboard and nut are ebony. The Benedetto S-6 pickup is a "floating" design, which does not make contact with the top.*

(COURTESY DALE RABINER)

Right: *A partly completed body for a Benedetto La Venezia, showing the X-bracing on the top.*

(COURTESY ROBERT BENEDETTO)

Right: *Benedetto Manhattan (16-inch) in shaded green "jazz-burst" finish. This guitar was custom-made for Bob Benedetto's daughter, Gina. It has since been played by many of the luthier's endorsees, and was used by Andy Summers (formerly of the UK rock group The Police) when he appeared at a concert featuring eight leading "Benedetto Players" in May 1997.*

(COURTESY GINA BENEDETTO)

Robert Benedetto –
Innovation and Tradition

Robert Benedetto produces a varied range of models, and has been influential in developing the seven-string guitar, which features an extra bass string tuned a fifth below the existing low E. The seven-string adaptation to an archtop guitar was introduced by the great jazz guitarist George Van Eps (b. 1913) in the 1930s, and has since been used by a growing number of leading players, such as Howard Alden, Bucky and John Pizzarelli, Ron Eschete, and Jimmy Bruno – all of whom own Benedetto guitars.

The picture below shows a customized seven-string made by Bob Benedetto for Jimmy Bruno, who was happy to let Bob make the essential decisions about its sound and feel. "The best thing to do with someone like Bob is to say, 'You make it the way you want to make it.' Who knows better than the guy who's making it what's going to sound better?" Seven-strings now account for about 25 per cent of Benedetto's archtop guitar output, making him the most prolific builder of the instrument.

In his long career as a luthier, Bob Benedetto has been responsible for a number of significant developments in archtop design. In 1982, he constructed a guitar without inlays or bindings for the late Chuck Wayne, setting a trend for simplicity and purity that was followed by many other makers. Bob has also introduced "honey blonde" finishes, ebony pickguards and tailpieces, and the innovative "Renaissance Series" of instruments with standard f-holes replaced by

Below: Benedetto seven-string guitar, custom-made for Jimmy Bruno. Its 17-inch (43.2cm) body is finished in honey blonde, and it has a floating Benedetto S-7 pickup with volume and tone controls mounted (almost invisibly) on the pickguard. The tailpiece inlay, showing Jimmy Bruno's name, is mother-of-pearl. (Courtesy Jimmy Bruno)

Left: The top of this guitar is made from sitka spruce, and the body is American maple with ebony fittings.

Left: *Benedetto Cremona (left-hand model). The 17-inch instrument takes its name from the town in Italy where the violin-maker Antonio Stradivari lived and worked. The top and back are carved from European tonewoods, and the flared, burl-veneered headstock is inlaid with mother-of-pearl and abalone.*
(COURTESY DALE RABINER)

unique, clustered sound openings (see page 148). However, he remains cautious of change for change's sake In his book, *Making an Archtop Guitar,* he reminds budding luthiers that "refinements, or so called improvements, are successful only when the player is involved. It is undeniably the player who will legitimize the maker's efforts." Significantly, Benedetto's highest accolades come from the musicians who use his instruments. These include Kenny Burrell, Cal Collins, Frank Vignola, Stéphane Grappelli (who played a Benedetto violin), and British guitarists Martin Taylor, Andy Summers, Andy MacKenzie, and Adrian Ingram.

Above and below: *Benedetto 25th Anniversary guitar. Made in 1993 to celebrate Bob Benedetto's then 25th year as a luthier. The shaded natural finish is a variation on Benedetto's signature "honey blonde" coloring, and the guitar is made from the finest European woods (spruce top, maple back). The burl veneer, also seen on the Cremona, is used here on the headstock, tuning buttons, pickguard, bridge base, and tailpiece.*
(COURTESY ROY MCDONALD; PHOTOGRAPH BY JONATHAN LEVIN)

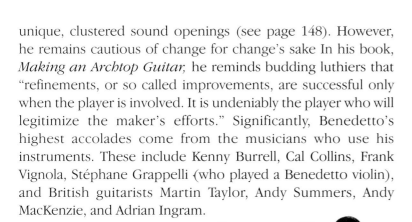

John Buscarino and Dale Unger

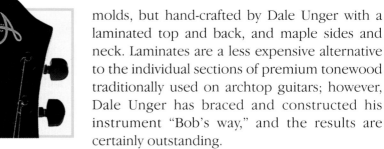

Twenty-five years ago, British guitarist Ivor Mairants wrote in the UK's *BMG* (Banjo, Mandolin & Guitar) magazine that the archtop guitar's days seemed to be numbered: "Most people hardly remember the instrument played by Eddie Lang... Development of it has almost stopped and until it again increases in popularity, very few makers will concentrate on its improvement." Thankfully, things have changed considerably since the early 1970s, and a wide range of first-class archtops is now being built and played. This healthy situation is at least partly due to the influence of luthiers like Bob Benedetto, John Monteleone, and the late Jimmy D'Aquisto, who have inspired younger guitar-builders to turn their attention to archtop construction.

Dale Unger, whose "American Dream" model is shown opposite, was born in 1954, and grew up in Nazareth, Pennsylvania, headquarters of the Martin Company. He has been strongly influenced by his contact with Martin craftsmen and guitars, and by a three-year period working with Bob Benedetto, who lives in nearby East Stroudsburg. The American Dream is made from Benedetto's patterns and molds, but hand-crafted by Dale Unger with a laminated top and back, and maple sides and neck. Laminates are a less expensive alternative to the individual sections of premium tonewood traditionally used on archtop guitars; however, Dale Unger has braced and constructed his instrument "Bob's way," and the results are certainly outstanding.

John Buscarino is another former Benedetto apprentice, who also studied with the leading classical guitar-maker Augustine LoPrinzi. Buscarino is now based in Florida, where he builds archtops, flat-tops and nylon-strung guitars (see page 149 for a photograph of his innovative "Cabaret" cutaway classical design). His instruments are hand-made from American and European woods, and are in strong demand from players and collectors – including the American guitar connoisseur Scott Chinery, for whom John made the "Blue Guitar" shown below. It is part of a group of 23 guitars (all blue 18-inch archtops) commissioned from leading luthiers which have been displayed at the Smithsonian Institution in Washington D.C.

Left and above: *"Blue Guitar" by John Buscarino. Like the other 22 guitars in the series commissioned by Scott Chinery, this is an 18-inch (45.7cm) archtop. Buscarino has embellished the fingerboard and tailpiece with striking vine inlays which provide a pleasing contrast with the blue body.* (COURTESY JOHN BUSCARINO)

Left and below: *"American Dream" archtop guitar by Dale Unger's "American Archtop" company. The instrument was built using Bob Benedetto's designs and molds. Its top and back are made from laminated woods, and it has a 17-inch (43.2cm) body with a 3-inch (7.62cm) depth. The logo on the headstock* **(opposite page, inset)** *was created by Dale Unger with Dick Boak from the Martin Guitar Company*

(COURTESY DALE UNGER/ROBERT BENEDETTO)

Modern American Archtops

The first guitar shown here has a fascinating history, and has traveled many thousands of miles from its "birthplace" in Toledo, Ohio (where it was built by W.G. Barker in 1964) to its current home with jazz guitarist Martin Taylor in Scotland. Originally destined for American jazz musician Howard Roberts, it was sold instead to a Hollywood studio guitarist, Johnny Gray, who used it on the soundtracks of many film and TV scores, including that of *Batman*. It can also be heard accompanying Elvis Presley's performance of "Love Me Tender." Subsequently, the instrument made its way to Australia, and was purchased and brought to London by Ike Issacs, guitarist with Stéphane Grappelli in the early 1970s. Issacs presented it to the young Martin Taylor as a 21st birthday present.

The other photographs feature two fine examples of 1990s archtops. Mark Campellone (b. 1954) from Providence, Rhode Island, studied at the famous Berklee College of Music in Boston, Massachusetts. He began his career as a luthier in the mid-1970s after several years' experience as a professional musician, and built his first archtop in 1988. Campellone's instruments are strongly influenced by the work of Gibson and other classic archtop makers; he works largely alone, and is entirely self-taught. He currently makes about 30 guitars a year, offering three models, the Standard, Deluxe, and Special (shown here). Like a number of guitar-makers featured in this chapter, he has recently contributed a "blue guitar" to Scott Chinery's famous collection.

Bruce Sexauer (b. 1947) based in Sausalito, California, is an experienced maker of many different types of stringed instruments – including dulcimers, mandolins, psalteries, and harps, as well as electric and acoustic guitars. He began his career as a luthier in 1967, and started making archtops in the late 1980s.

The Ensemble JZ-17 is the second-largest of his three regular models; he has also recently developed a "Coo'stic Dominator" guitar, which combines elements of archtop and Selmer-Maccaferri (Django Reinhardt-style) designs.

Below: *Campellone Special 17-inch (left-hand model). This guitar has a "thin-line" design, with a slimmer profile than most standard archtops. Its top is spruce, its back and sides maple, and its fingerboard ebony. The pickup, made by Ibanez in Japan, is a replica of the Gibson "Johnny Smith" model.*
(COURTESY DALE RABINER)

Opposite page: *Bruce Sexauer JZ-17. This "Ensemble" model (Sexauer also makes "Personal" and "Soloist" instruments with differing woods and finishes) has an Englemann spruce top, with a maple back and sides. The neck is also maple, and the headstock decorations are inlaid with ebony and mother-of-pearl.* (COURTESY ERIC SCHOENBERG)

Below and opposite page, inset: *Guitar by W.G. Barker, Toledo, Ohio, 1964. The distinctively shaped headstock has its present owner Martin Taylor's name inlaid on the truss-rod cover. The instrument's original metal tailpiece was replaced at Martin Taylor's request; the new one, which is ebony, was provided by Bob Benedetto.*

(COURTESY MARTIN TAYLOR)

CHAPTER 5
AMERICAN FLAT-TOPS

*I*n 1922, the same year that Gibson introduced the L-5 archtop, the Martin Company first fitted steel strings as standard to its model 2-17 flat-top guitar. This important move was probably hastened by the huge popularity of Hawaiian groups during the 1920s. Martin was already making a considerable number of the specially-adapted steel-strung guitars played by these musicians, and the transition to using steel on its regular models was relatively easy. The next year, steel strings were offered on Martin's Style 18 guitars, and Style 28 followed suit in 1925.

Like Gibson, Martin had been experimenting with bigger bodies in order to boost the sound and projection of its guitars – although it never built an instrument as large as the 18-inch Orville-styles. At the turn of the century, Martin's widest body was "size 00," which measured 14⅛in (35.9cm). In 1902, the company launched the 15-inch (38.1cm) 000, and although guitars made in this size were initially slow sellers, they became increasingly popular in the early 1920s.

Soon afterwards, the 000 was the starting point for a significant design modification. It was inspired by Perry Bechtel, a leading banjoist planning to make the transition to the guitar, who approached Martin with a request for a flat-top that he would find more manageable to play. In particular, he wanted a narrower neck, and easier access to the higher reaches of the fingerboard. Martin responded by squaring off the top of the 000's body to accommodate a re-shaped and repositioned neck, which joined the body at the 14th fret. (Previous Martins followed classical guitar design, and had necks with only 12 frets easily accessible.) The new instrument, named the OM (Orchestra Model), was launched in 1930.

Fourteen-fret necks eventually became the norm not just on Martin flat-tops, but on their competitors' instruments too (they were already in regular use on archtop guitars). Martin's next major innovation, the large "Dreadnought"-size body, was also widely imitated. It was derived from a design the company had previously manufactured for the Boston-based Ditson retail chain, and its impressively bulky

shape led to its being named after a famous class of battleship. Dreadnoughts quickly became the instruments of choice among players who needed the extra power they provided, and they are especially favored by folk and country music guitarists.

Below: *Martin O.M-45, 1933. The O.M version of Style 45 was introduced in 1930. The difference in body shape between this guitar and the 000-45 – the result of Perry Bechtel's request for an instrument with different dimensions – can be clearly seen. The neck now joins the body at the 14th fret.*

(COURTESY MARTIN GUITAR COMPANY)

Above: Martin 000-45, 1929. This model features pearl inlays on its fingerboard, around its soundhole and sides, and adjoining the top and neck. It has 12 frets clear of its body.
(COURTESY MARTIN TAYLOR)

Below: Martin D-28, 1945. The rosewood-bodied D-28 first appeared in 1931. This model is one of the last instruments of its period to feature Martin's distinctive "herringbone" decoration around its top. (COURTESY ERIC SCHOENBERG)

The decoration was discontinued, due to shortage of supplies, in 1946, but has since been reintroduced thanks to customer demand.

Martin – A Dynasty of Flat-top Designs

artin is the longest-established and most consistently successful guitar-maker in the USA, and the company's flat-tops retain close links with the designs of its founder, C.F. Martin Sr. In the 1850s, he developed a system of X-bracing for the tops of his instruments, giving sweet-sounding results on the gut-strung guitars of the time. Later, when X-braces were combined with steel strings, they helped to create the "trademark" Martin sound – a rich, singing tone very different from the more cutting, less sustained quality of most archtop guitars. X-bracing is, of course, still in use today, as are several of the instrument "styles" from the turn of the century or earlier. Two of the guitars illustrated are Style 28s, with spruce top, rosewood back and sides, and Martin's famous "herringbone" trim around their edges; the first recorded example of this design appeared in 1870. The third instrument is an OM-45; the model dates from 1930, but the blueprint for Style 45 dates from 1904. Styles 28 and 45 both remain in Martin's current catalog with some minor changes.

Below: Martin 000-28, 1929. Martin's OM (Orchestra Model) was officially introduced in 1930 – but the rare instrument shown here was part of an initial batch of only 12 "OM-style" models produced in 1929, before the new classification was in use.

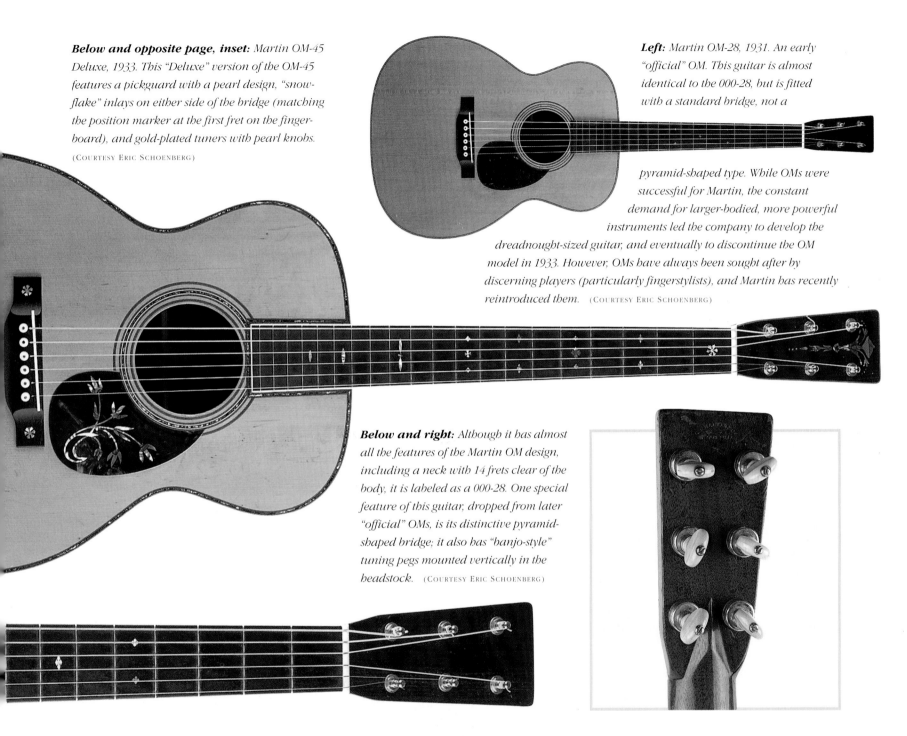

Below and opposite page, inset: *Martin OM-45 Deluxe, 1933. This "Deluxe" version of the OM-45 features a pickguard with a pearl design, "snow-flake" inlays on either side of the bridge (matching the position marker at the first fret on the finger-board), and gold-plated tuners with pearl knobs.* (COURTESY ERIC SCHOENBERG)

Left: *Martin OM-28, 1931. An early "official" OM. This guitar is almost identical to the 000-28, but is fitted with a standard bridge, not a pyramid-shaped type. While OMs were successful for Martin, the constant demand for larger-bodied, more powerful instruments led the company to develop the dreadnought-sized guitar, and eventually to discontinue the OM model in 1933. However, OMs have always been sought after by discerning players (particularly fingerstylists), and Martin has recently reintroduced them.* (COURTESY ERIC SCHOENBERG)

Below and right: *Although it has almost all the features of the Martin OM design, including a neck with 14 frets clear of the body, it is labeled as a 000-28. One special feature of this guitar, dropped from later "official" OMs, is its distinctive pyramid-shaped bridge; it also has "banjo-style" tuning pegs mounted vertically in the headstock.* (COURTESY ERIC SCHOENBERG)

Martin is a family business, and C.F. Martin's descendants have always retained control over it. For some 57 years between 1888 and about 1945, the founder's grandson, Frank Henry Martin (1866–1948), ran the company. He took over from his father, C.F. Martin Jr., and saw the firm through times of exciting opportunity, changing demand, economic depression, and world war. Thanks to his guidance, Martin profited from the good times and survived the bad ones. It was active in other areas of instrument building, establishing successful mandolin and ukulele lines, and making short-lived attempts at archtop guitar and banjo manufacture, but continued to focus most of its energies on its core activity – the development of the flat-top. By the 1930s, the company had a flourishing range of small and larger-bodied guitars, and also undertook custom design work. This area was soon to grow in importance, as other star names followed Perry Bechtel in requesting specially modified and "personalized" instruments to suit their own needs.

Martin's "Special Projects"

Unlike some other guitar-makers, Martin has never made direct endorsement deals with its players. However, it does undertake "special projects" in conjunction with some performers, and one of the most famous of these is the collaboration with the "Singing Cowboy," Gene Autry (b. 1907). Autry had played Martin Style 42 guitars while he was still working as an Oklahoma telegraph operator in the mid-1920s. In 1933, after he found fame and fortune, he ordered one of the new Martin Dreadnoughts in Style 45, asking for his name to be inlaid in pearl on the fingerboard. At the time, Dreadnoughts were only built in Style 18 (mahogany body) and Style 28 (rosewood body), but Martin created a D-45 especially for Autry, and subsequently produced the guitar (without the custom inlay) as a regular model.

Making the Autry D-45 was an exception to Martin's normal policy. As the company's current Chairman, Chris Martin IV, explains, "Our models are so well known, and it's not so much that we create a new model as adapt an existing one." This approach was followed in 1995, when Eric Clapton collaborated with Martin on a limited edition 000-42 with a number of other special features. Only 461 were made (the figure commemorates Clapton's 1974 "comeback" album, "461 Ocean Boulevard"), but the project was so successful that Martin went on to develop a "stock" Eric Clapton model, the 000-28EC, which is currently available in its "Vintage" series. Other leading musicians who have given their names to special Martin guitars include Paul Simon, country rock star Marty Stuart, Joan Baez and Sting.

A very small number of Martins are "one-of-a-kind" custom creations kept on permanent display at the firm's factory in Nazareth. These include the Stauffer-style reissue with inlaid illustrations, made to commemorate the 200th anniversary of the founder's birth (see pages 48-49), as well as the 500,000th instrument to be produced by the company. This is an HD-28 Dreadnought, built in 1990, and signed by the entire workforce (see opposite).

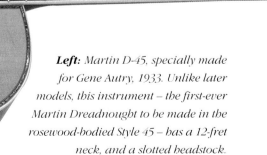

Left: Martin D-45, specially made for Gene Autry, 1933. Unlike later models, this instrument – the first-ever Martin Dreadnought to be made in the rosewood-bodied Style 45 – has a 12-fret neck, and a slotted headstock.
(COURTESY AUTRY MUSEUM OF WESTERN HERITAGE)

Right: *Martin HD-28, 1990. This guitar was the 500,000th instrument to be completed by Martin, and has been signed by the entire staff. It is now on display at the company's museum in its Nazareth, Pennsylvania headquarters. The "H" prefix refers to the herringbone trim – a favorite Martin feature dropped after World War II, but reintroduced in 1976.*

(COURTESY MARTIN GUITAR COMPANY)

Left: *Martin 000-42EC, 1995. Eric Clapton played an active part in the development of this limited edition guitar – only 461 were made. The top is spruce, the body East Indian rosewood; the instrument also features a beveled pickguard, and two pearl "snowflakes" on its bridge.*

(COURTESY MARTIN GUITAR COMPANY)

Gibson's First Flat-tops

*I*t took some time for Gibson to approach Martin's level of commitment to the flat-top. It did not enter the market until 1926, when it launched only two models: one of these, the L-1, "borrowed" its name from a previous Gibson archtop (seen earlier on pages 56-57), and was issued with a cheaper companion, the L-0. Gibson's third flat-top, which appeared in 1928, was endorsed by the American vaudeville and cabaret performer Nick Lucas. Six years earlier, Lucas (1897–1982) had recorded some of the first jazz-influenced guitar solos, including the classic "Teasin' The Frets," and in 1929 he went on to even greater success with his multi-million-selling hit, "Tiptoe Through the Tulips." The Lucas guitar was popular, despite its high price ($125); and over the next few years, Gibson's flat-top range started to make

Below: Gibson Nick Lucas (reissue). A modern replica, made by Gibson, of its first top-quality flat-top guitar, launched in 1928. It has a spruce top, and back and sides of maple. The original model had 12 frets clear of its body, but by the mid-1930s it had been fitted with a 14-fret neck like the one shown here.

(COURTESY MANDOLIN BROTHERS, NEW YORK)

an impact as the company responded to Martin's OMs and Dreadnoughts with some innovations of their own.

In 1934, Gibson launched a large-bodied flat-top, the "Jumbo." The original model was superseded in 1936 by two new guitars, the "Advanced Jumbo" and the "Jumbo 35." All three instruments were 16in (40.6cm) wide, with 14 frets clear of their bodies. Like Martin's Dreadnoughts, they featured X-braced tops, but were slightly shallower-bodied and more "round-shouldered" than their rivals. They were competitively priced: the Advanced Jumbo sold for $80 and the J-35 for only $35. (Martin's D-28 Dreadnought cost $100 in 1935, while Gibson's own top-of-the-line archtop guitar was priced at $400.) The Gibson Jumbo range (the name would eventually be taken up by many other manufacturers of larger flat-tops) was later expanded, as the Advanced Jumbo gave way to the Super Jumbo (SJ), a model which is still available today.

Gibson also introduced a number of cheaper instruments during the early 1930s. The most basic model was the L-00, which appeared in the company's 1932 catalog and remained in production until the end of World War II. Early examples of this guitar, like the one shown here, had a black finish, and are thought to be the first Gibsons ever issued in a single color.

Left: Gibson L-00, 1934. The L-00 was introduced in about 1931 as the most basic model in Gibson's "L" range of small-bodied flat-tops. It sold for $37.50, and later the price was reduced to $30. Its back, sides, and neck are mahogany, with a spruce top and a rosewood fingerboard.

(Courtesy Real Guitars, San Francisco)

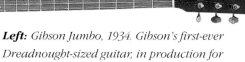

Above: The "fleur-de-lys" inlay is a 1930s-style feature of the Gibson Nick Lucas.

Right: The company's 1934 catalog describes the advantages of the Gibson Jumbo's larger body: "[It] produces a heavy, booming tone so popular with many players who do vocal or small combination accompaniment…the bass of this model will amaze you, and of course the clear, brilliant treble is in perfect balance."

(Courtesy Mandolin Brothers, New York)

Left: Gibson Jumbo, 1934. Gibson's first-ever Dreadnought-sized guitar, in production for only two years (1934–1936).

The Gibson "Super Jumbo" Range

Gibson's "Super Jumbo" line evolved from a collaboration with "cowboy" singing star Ray Whitley, a major figure in pre-war radio and films. The instrument he helped to develop, which came to be known as the SJ-200, first appeared in the stores in 1938. It was named, like many Gibsons, after its price ($200), and its lavishly decorated body, originally 16⅞ inches (42.9cm) in width, was later enlarged to 17 inches (43.2cm). It had a more pronounced waist than Gibson's previous Jumbos, a distinctive, pearl-inlaid "mustache" bridge, and a large pickguard engraved with flowers and vines. The guitar stayed in limited production throughout the war years, and in 1947 it was rechristened the J-200. It remains one of the most instantly recognizable and respected of all Gibson flat-tops. The many leading artists associated with it include Elvis Presley, Emmylou Harris, Rick Nelson, and bluesman Rev. Gary Davis – who used to refer to his J-200 as "Miss Gibson".

In 1942, another Gibson "SJ" instrument appeared. Confusingly, its initials stood not for "Super Jumbo" but "Southerner Jumbo" – a 16-inch (40.6cm) ,mahogany-bodied flat-top (although some wartime models had backs and sides made from maple) that remained in the catalog, with minor alterations, for over 30 years. Among its devotees were the Everly Brothers, who featured it on several of their hit records, including "Wake Up, Little Susie." In 1954, Gibson introduced a natural-color version; this was renamed the "Country-Western" two years later, and is shown opposite.

The third instrument illustrated here, a B-25, dates from the early 1960s, and was specially selected for its owner, Derrick Weskin, by the distinguished British jazz guitarist John McLaughlin, who was working behind the counter at a London guitar store at the time! The 1960s were a particularly successful decade for Gibson, thanks to the folk music boom and the impact of high-profile Gibson users such as the Beatles. Unfortunately, the next period in the company's history was a less happy one; the problems faced by Gibson in the 1970s and early 1980s, and the way these have now been solved, are discussed in Section Three.

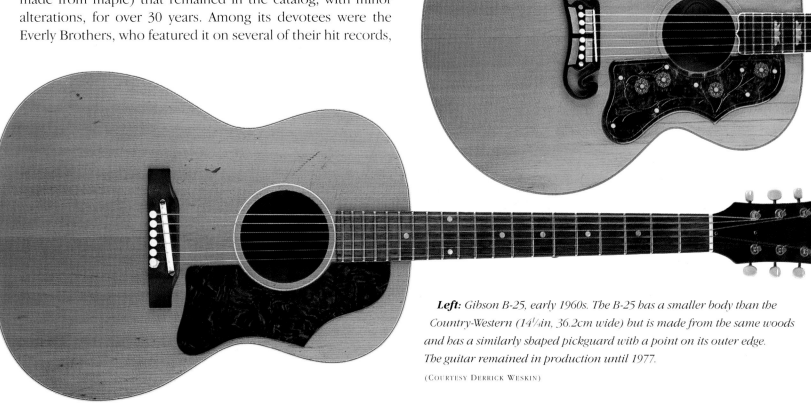

Left: *Gibson B-25, early 1960s. The B-25 has a smaller body than the Country-Western (14¼in, 36.2cm wide) but is made from the same woods and has a similarly shaped pickguard with a point on its outer edge. The guitar remained in production until 1977.*

(COURTESY DERRICK WESKIN)

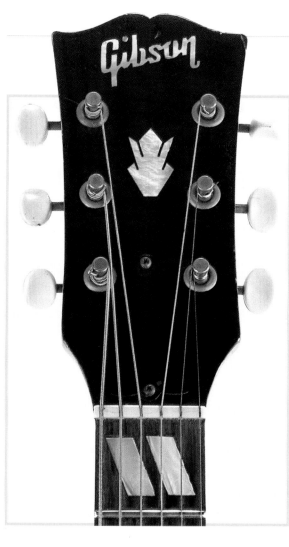

Left and right: *Gibson Country-Western Jumbo, 1959. This natural-finish version of the Gibson Southerner Jumbo has a spruce top and mahogany back and sides.*

The guitar features a rosewood fingerboard displaying the company's distinctive "double parallelogram" inlays, which are also seen on many Gibson electrics.

(COURTESY DERRICK WESKIN)

Center left: *Gibson SJ-200, 1950. Its top is spruce, its back and sides are maple. Among the SJ-200's many striking features are its elaborate bridge, with four rectangular pearl inlays above and below the string-pins, the "crest" fingerboard markers (similar to the "cloud" inlays first used in the 1930s by Gibson's competitors, Epiphone), and the beautiful hand-carved pickguard.*

(COURTESY HANK'S, LONDON)

Santa Cruz: Californian Craftsmanship

One of the most important developments in the recent history of flat-top guitar building has been the emergence of a number of small, dedicated companies committed to the highest standards of workmanship and design. They often draw inspiration from the work of earlier makers, but are also keen to introduce their own improvements and innovations, and able to tailor their instruments closely to the requirements of their customers. Richard Hoover, of Santa Cruz, California, was one of the first American luthiers to set up such a firm. He began making guitars during the early 1970s, working alone in his garage, and explains that "in building on my own, I saw an impossible learning-curve ahead of me – years and years of experimenting to come up with the perfect guitar." Richard decided to take on two partners, and together they formed the Santa Cruz Guitar Company. "My intent was to have each of us specialize in a certain aspect of guitar building, so that we could accelerate the learning process and make more guitars, while keeping to the principle of the individual luthier having control over each aspect of building."

This philosophy has created a thriving business. Richard Hoover now runs the Santa Cruz Guitar Company himself, employing 11 guitar-makers and six other staff. There is no assembly line; the builders work closely together on what Richard describes as "a logical series of processes that contribute to the whole; they can understand what they've done and how it affects the guitar." Santa Cruz produces 15 basic models, and its instruments have been associated with leading players such as Eric Clapton and bluegrass guitarist Doc Watson.

The company's close relationship with a second major name in bluegrass, Tony Rice, led to the creation of the Santa Cruz Tony Rice Model (illustrated). This is based on the classic Martin Dreadnought, but offers a more balanced response than the original 1930s D-28, which had a powerful bass but less treble and mid-range presence. Also shown here are two versions of another Santa Cruz guitar derived from a pre-War Martin design: their OM (Orchestra Model).

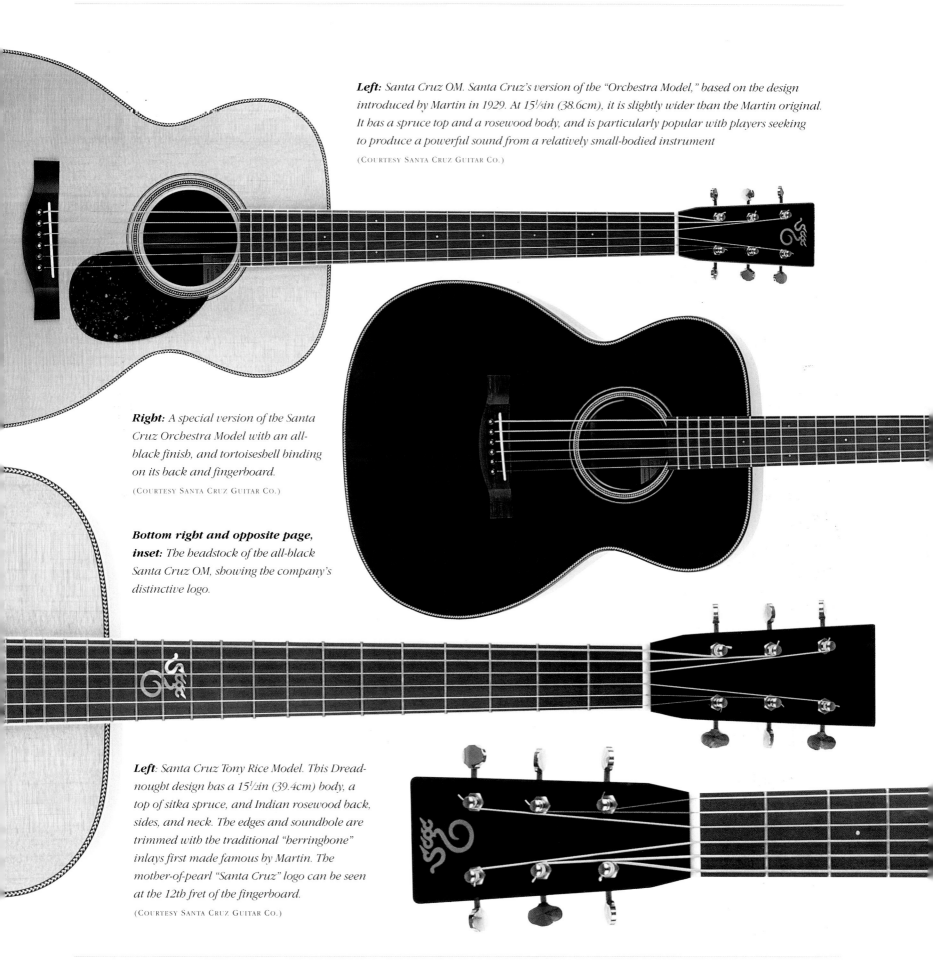

Left: *Santa Cruz OM. Santa Cruz's version of the "Orchestra Model," based on the design introduced by Martin in 1929. At 15⅛in (38.6cm), it is slightly wider than the Martin original. It has a spruce top and a rosewood body, and is particularly popular with players seeking to produce a powerful sound from a relatively small-bodied instrument* (COURTESY SANTA CRUZ GUITAR CO.)

Right: *A special version of the Santa Cruz Orchestra Model with an all-black finish, and tortoiseshell binding on its back and fingerboard.* (COURTESY SANTA CRUZ GUITAR CO.)

Bottom right and opposite page, inset: *The headstock of the all-black Santa Cruz OM, showing the company's distinctive logo.*

Left: *Santa Cruz Tony Rice Model. This Dreadnought design has a 15½in (39.4cm) body, a top of sitka spruce, and Indian rosewood back, sides, and neck. The edges and soundhole are trimmed with the traditional "herringbone" inlays first made famous by Martin. The mother-of-pearl "Santa Cruz" logo can be seen at the 12th fret of the fingerboard.* (COURTESY SANTA CRUZ GUITAR CO.)

Santa Cruz: Anatomy of a Flat-top

Santa Cruz's first reworkings of vintage Martin styles were one-off custom orders for individual clients. But their guitars attracted so much interest that Richard Hoover eventually added them to the company's regular catalog. "Not only were these guitars in demand, but they were also really nice designs. At the time, Martin wasn't making them, so there was a lot of pent-up demand." Richard acknowledges the importance of Martin's influence on his own development as a player and luthier, and is proud that the appearance of Santa Cruz 000s and OMs has encouraged Martin to restart production of these classic models themselves.

Like nearly all serious producers of flat-top guitars, Santa Cruz uses X-bracing on its instruments. The tops themselves are made from sitka or German spruce, which is carefully selected and evaluated; more flexible wood tends to accentuate the guitar's bass response, while greater rigidity will boost the mid-range and treble. The positioning of the braces helps to "tailor" the sound of the instrument by stiffening some areas of the top, making them more responsive to higher frequencies, and the completed structure is sometimes lined with basswood to isolate it from the guitar's sides and back. Other factors influencing the overall tonal quality of the guitar include the size of the soundhole (a larger hole raises the fundamental frequency of the body, giving more mid-range and treble) and the selection of woods used for other parts of the guitar.

Santa Cruz instruments are a blend of tradition and innovation, and the company's pioneering approach to the business of guitar-making has since been followed by several other firms. Looking back over more than two decades as a luthier, Richard Hoover observes that "for the most part, there used to be nothing between the single builder and the factory. That's the niche we want to fill – to be a small company that is building superior instruments and really responsive to the players' needs."

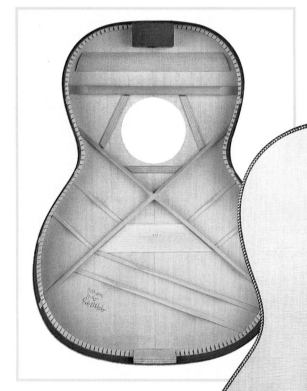

Above: *This picture of the inside of the body of a Santa Cruz 000 under construction shows the central X-brace and the reinforcing struts.*

Left: *The headstock of the Santa Cruz Model F illustrated on the opposite page bears the distinctive company logo.*

Left: *Santa Cruz Model F twelve-string. This instrument is built from European woods: German spruce for the top, and maple for the back, neck, and sides.*

(Courtesy Santa Cruz Guitar Co.)

Right: *Santa Cruz Model F cutaway. Both the six- and twelve-string Model Fs have headstocks based on Epiphone's classic "asymmetrical" design (see pages 62-63 for the Epiphone originals). The six-string, made from spruce and rosewood, has a custom binding of Hawaiian koa wood.*

(Courtesy Santa Cruz Guitar Co.)

Left: *Santa Cruz 000 (12-fret model). Another outstanding reworking of a classic Martin design, with a spruce top, and Indian rosewood back, sides, and neck. The top is fitted with a central X-brace, as well as additional strutting to provide further stiffening and strength. The edges are lined with glued-in strips of basswood.*

(Courtesy Santa Cruz Guitar Co.)

Bob Taylor – High Technology and Fine Design

*I*n 1974, a young Californian luthier, Bob Taylor, started a guitar-making business with a colleague, Kurt Listug, in a small shop in Lemon Grove, near San Diego. The company they created, Taylor Guitars, has developed a unique, innovative approach to instrument building, combining traditional craftsmanship with high technology. Today, it is a major force in the industry, with almost 70,000sq ft (6,500m²) of factory space in El Cajon, California, a daily output of 100 guitars, and an enviable reputation among leading players throughout the world.

Among the many major performers associated with Taylor's instruments are Nanci Griffith, Kenny Loggins, Jewel, Kathy Mattea, Iris DeMent, Bonnie Raitt, Neil Young, and the late John Denver. Bill Clinton also has a Taylor; in 1997, the company presented him with a commemorative guitar (bearing his Inaugural Seal on the headstock) to mark his re-election to the US Presidency.

Bob Taylor's own innovative approach to lutherie lies at the heart of the company's success. His skills have enabled him to create viable designs from unlikely materials such as "junk" timber from an abandoned pallet (see illustration), although for production models, he is committed to working with fine quality solid tonewoods. To manufacture his guitars, Bob makes use of Computer Numeric Control (CNC) systems, which drive machinery capable of cutting, carving, and planing at speeds and tolerances no human craftsman could match. CNC's precision removes the inevitable inconsistencies that occur when working by hand, allowing Bob and his staff to "get closer to actually producing what it is we had in mind." It also enables them to make even intricately carved or decorated parts quickly and in considerable numbers. However, as Bob emphasizes, this impressive technology is simply a means to an end: "We're guitar builders first. Choice of tools [comes] second, and we're very comfortable with high-technology tools to make a low-technology product. [CNC] makes us more consistent and more efficient, so that we can deliver more guitars to people at reasonable prices that really give them what they're hoping to have when they play that guitar."

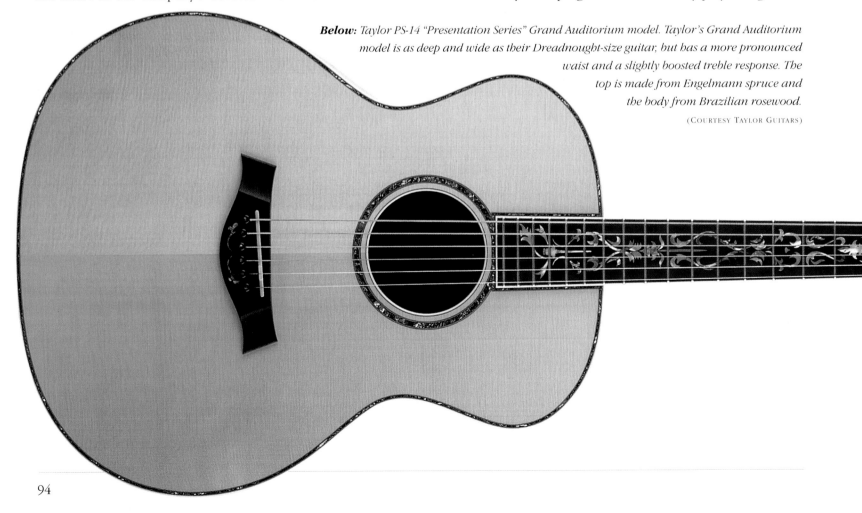

Below: *Taylor PS-14 "Presentation Series" Grand Auditorium model. Taylor's Grand Auditorium model is as deep and wide as their Dreadnought-size guitar, but has a more pronounced waist and a slightly boosted treble response. The top is made from Engelmann spruce and the body from Brazilian rosewood.*

(COURTESY TAYLOR GUITARS)

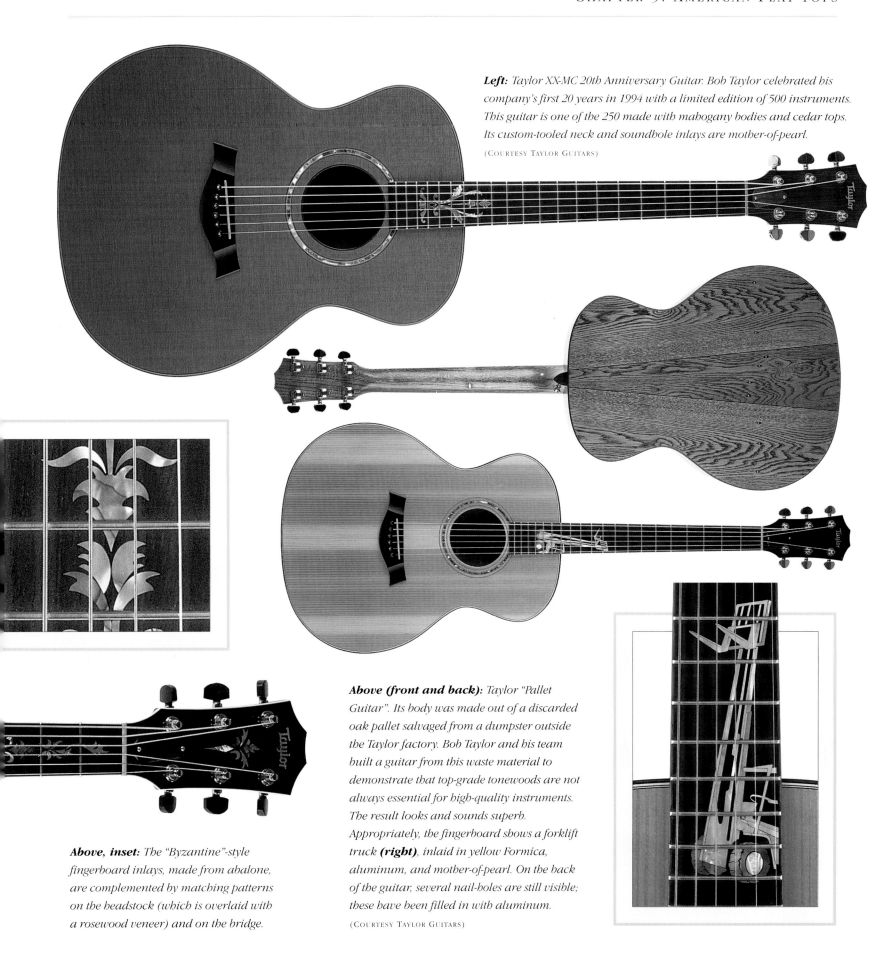

Left: *Taylor XX-MC 20th Anniversary Guitar. Bob Taylor celebrated his company's first 20 years in 1994 with a limited edition of 500 instruments. This guitar is one of the 250 made with mahogany bodies and cedar tops. Its custom-tooled neck and soundhole inlays are mother-of-pearl.*

(COURTESY TAYLOR GUITARS)

Above, inset: *The "Byzantine"-style fingerboard inlays, made from abalone, are complemented by matching patterns on the headstock (which is overlaid with a rosewood veneer) and on the bridge.*

Above (front and back): *Taylor "Pallet Guitar". Its body was made out of a discarded oak pallet salvaged from a dumpster outside the Taylor factory. Bob Taylor and his team built a guitar from this waste material to demonstrate that top-grade tonewoods are not always essential for high-quality instruments. The result looks and sounds superb. Appropriately, the fingerboard shows a forklift truck **(right)**, inlaid in yellow Formica, aluminum, and mother-of-pearl. On the back of the guitar, several nail-holes are still visible; these have been filled in with aluminum.*

(COURTESY TAYLOR GUITARS)

Bob Taylor – The "Cujo" and Leo Kottke Models

Taylor's limited edition "Cujo" guitar is the product of two years' painstaking preparation and design. The instrument takes its name from Stephen King's 1981 novel, in which Cujo, a St. Bernard dog, is bitten by a rabid bat and becomes a crazed predator. The story was filmed in 1983 on a Californian ranch, and wood from a black walnut tree that grew there and was seen in the movie has been used to make 250 special guitars, each signed by Stephen King himself. The elaborate fingerboard decorations on these instruments, showing images related to the story, were all inlaid using computer numeric control. The fine detail achieved by the automated system would be difficult enough for a skilled engraver to match on a single custom guitar, let alone a production run of 250.

The CNC process turns out a series of perfect realizations of an original design; Bob Taylor points out that "every one's a master – none of them is a copy." In the development of that design, however, the emphasis is on traditional methods: experience, experimentation, and consultation with players. While working with bluegrass musician Dan Crary on the Taylor guitar that carries his name, Bob and his team assembled a pair of rough prototypes, replacing tops, altering bracing patterns, and making constant comparisons and adjustments in order to achieve the sound Crary wanted. The

creation of Leo Kottke's Signature Model twelve-string involved about four years of discussion with the artist. Such processes remain central to Taylor's approach to guitar building, and can never be replaced by technology.

The company's future plans focus on further refinements and improvements to the design and production of their instruments. Bob Taylor explains that "I still enjoy the traditional look and feel of what a guitar is. But what we'll be doing over the next five or ten years is redesigning the way a guitar goes together to really exploit the precision that we have at our disposal. I've been trying to do this for 20 years, and it's only now that I have the equipment to do it with."

Above right : *Taylor Leo Kottke Signature Model twelve-string cutaway. This guitar has a sitka spruce top, mahogany back, sides, and neck, and an ebony fingerboard. It is fitted with heavy-gauge strings, and is designed to be tuned a 3rd lower than normal.*

(COURTESY TAYLOR GUITARS)

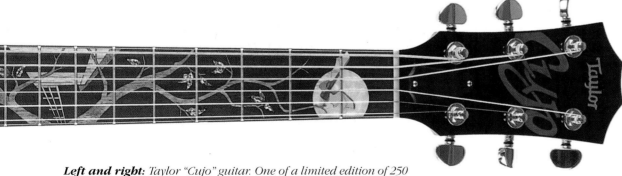

Left and right: *Taylor "Cujo" guitar. One of a limited edition of 250 instruments made from the wood of the walnut tree featured in the film of Stephen King's novel. The fingerboard depicts a bat silhouetted against a full moon; the branches of the walnut tree; the barn from where Cujo the dog launches his crazed attacks; and Cujo himself. The inlays were created using mahogany, maple, walnut, green heart abalone, black oyster shell, and Formica.*

(COURTESY TAYLOR GUITARS)

Eric Schoenberg – Growing Towards The Past

Eric Schoenberg brings a player's perspective to the art of guitar design. Since the 1960s, he has been searching for an instrument that would measure up to his own musical and technical needs, and the Schoenberg Soloist and its successors are the results of this quest.

As a distinguished performer of ragtime transcriptions and other elaborate fingerstyle arrangements, Eric Schoenberg's first requirement was for a guitar that would respond sympathetically to the subtleties of his technique. His initial choice, a Martin 000-45 with a 12-fret neck, could not provide the unrestricted access to the higher frets that he needed. He changed to a 14-fret 000-45, but found its scale length unsuitable. His next instrument solved the problem: "I ended up playing a Martin OM, and never found anything like it." The OM design, introduced in 1930 in response to a request from banjoist Perry Bechtel (see pages 80-81) offers a slightly modified 000-style shape and a long-scale neck with 14 frets clear of the body. Eric continued to use it for several years.

Below: Schoenberg 000-28K. Modeled on Martin's 1923 000-28 guitar, and made from koa wood.

(COURTESY ERIC SCHOENBERG)

Eventually, though, he began to consider the possibility of creating a new guitar, combining the features of the original OM with a cutaway to make the top frets even easier to reach. The Schoenberg Soloist, designed with luthier Dana Bourgeois, was the embodiment of these ideas, and it first appeared in 1986. For the next seven years, Soloists were built at the Martin factory in Nazareth, Pennsylvania, with Eric and Dana supplying the wood, the tops and bracing, the bridges, and the binding for the bodies.

Eric Schoenberg's subsequent design projects have been undertaken in partnership with Massachusetts guitar-maker Julius Borges. Their first production model was a replica of a 1923-style Martin 000-28, made in Hawaiian koa wood. More recently, they have realized what Eric describes as "one of my goals for years:" the creation of the Schoenberg Standard, a 12-fret 000 with a cutaway, offering an ideal combination of neck dimensions and fret access. Other instruments from Schoenberg Guitars include 12- and 14-fret 00 cutaways – further examples of Eric's policy of "backwards-looking innovation...learning from the past and growing towards it."

Left: *Schoenberg Soloist. Designed by Eric Schoenberg and Dana Bourgeois, and built at the Martin factory in Nazareth, Pennsylvania, to their specifications. Schoenbergs were made at Martin between 1986–1993.*

(COURTESY ERIC SCHOENBERG)

Right: *Schoenberg Standard (prototype), 1996. An instrument based on Martin's 12-fret 000-design, but featuring a cutaway to improve access to the upper frets. This is one of the recent batch of Schoenberg instruments made in Massachusetts in collaboration with luthier Julius Borges.*

(COURTESY ERIC SCHOENBERG)

Steve Klein – A Fresh Approach to the Flat-top

Steve Klein, of Sonoma, California, is widely regarded as one of the most innovative luthiers on the current American scene. His instruments are strikingly radical in both appearance and construction; he has a highly individual approach to bracing, bridge design, and choice of materials, using traditional woods alongside "space-age" substances such as carbon fiber to create guitars with a distinctive sound and feel.

Klein guitars are built by Steve and his fellow-luthier Steve Kauffman, who constructs the instrument bodies. Klein himself produces fretwork and inlays, makes the bridges, and undertakes the final assembly. Unusually, no X-bracing is used: instead, each top features a "flying brace" (inspired by the flying buttresses used in European cathedral architecture) combined with a series of fan-braces that overlap the edge of the "impedance-matching" bridge. The bridge itself, which is in two pieces, is significantly broader on its bass side. Steve Klein explains the reason for this: "What the bass and treble strings are trying to drive the top to do are quite different. You've got a much larger wave-pattern happening in the bass frequencies – so the wider bass side causes a much slower and broader pumping motion to the top." The separation and balance provided by the bridge contribute to the tonal clarity of the instrument, and Steve describes it as "the heart of the Klein acoustic."

Steve Klein makes four basic models of flat-top guitar, the L-45.7, M-43, S-39.6 and N-35.6 (the numbers refer to the width, in centimeters, of the body's lower bout), and also provides custom inlay work for many of his clients' instruments. The guitar he built for Canadian singer-songwriter Joni Mitchell featured mother-of-pearl I Ching symbols and other personalized images, while the cutaway model shown opposite includes elaborate "mushroom" inlays. His L-45.7s are high-end instruments, "not the kind of guitars that people take out on the road," as Steve comments; but the many leading players who use them regularly for studio and high-profile concert and broadcast work include Steve Miller and Andy Summers, as well as Joni Mitchell. In contrast, Klein's new M-43 guitars are designed with the touring musician in mind, and are priced in the $5,000-$6,000 range, with pickups installed.

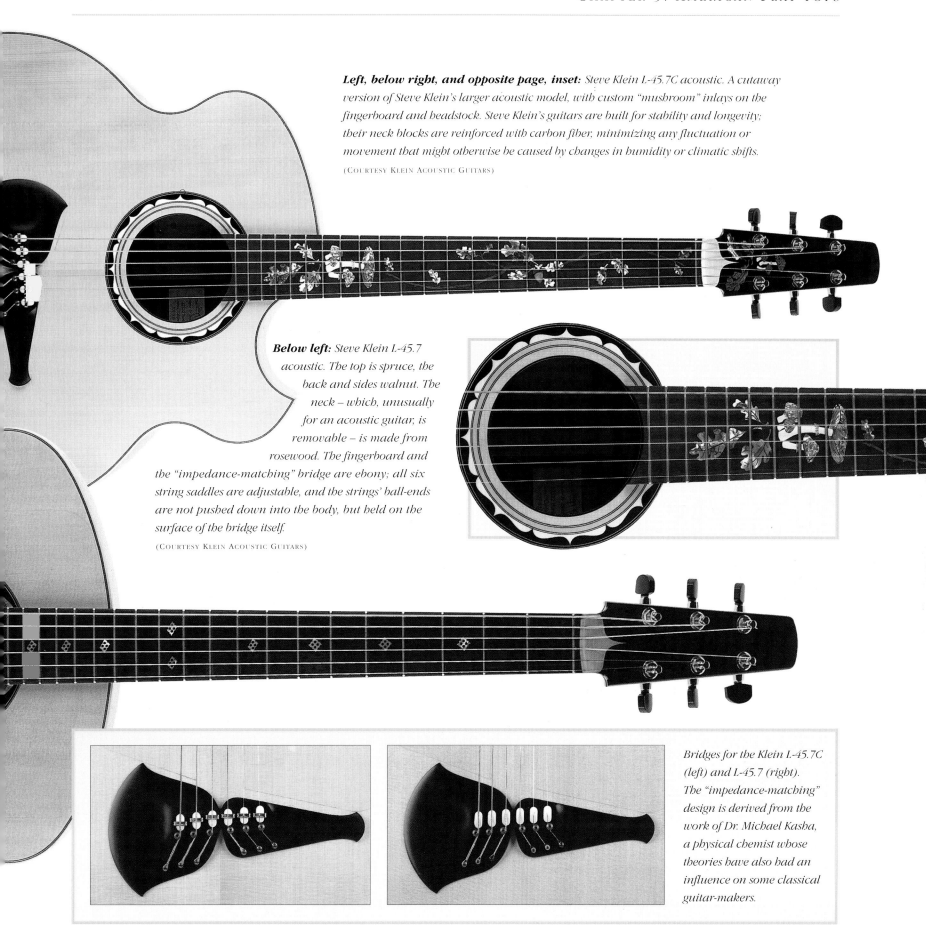

Left, below right, and opposite page, inset: *Steve Klein L-45.7C acoustic. A cutaway version of Steve Klein's larger acoustic model, with custom "mushroom" inlays on the fingerboard and headstock. Steve Klein's guitars are built for stability and longevity; their neck blocks are reinforced with carbon fiber, minimizing any fluctuation or movement that might otherwise be caused by changes in humidity or climatic shifts.*

(COURTESY KLEIN ACOUSTIC GUITARS)

Below left: *Steve Klein L-45.7 acoustic. The top is spruce, the back and sides walnut. The neck – which, unusually for an acoustic guitar, is removable – is made from rosewood. The fingerboard and the "impedance-matching" bridge are ebony; all six string saddles are adjustable, and the strings' ball-ends are not pushed down into the body, but held on the surface of the bridge itself.*

(COURTESY KLEIN ACOUSTIC GUITARS)

Bridges for the Klein L-45.7C (left) and L-45.7 (right). The "impedance-matching" design is derived from the work of Dr. Michael Kasha, a physical chemist whose theories have also had an influence on some classical guitar-makers.

Modern American Flat-tops

The great archtop luthier Jimmy D'Aquisto (1935–1995) started making flat-tops as the result of a mistake by one of his suppliers. After receiving a consignment of German flat-top woods that had been delivered to his workshop in error, he began developing a number of unusual design ideas for the instrument, and went on to build flat-top guitars for Paul Simon, Janis Ian, and other well-known names. The model shown here, the "Forté," dates from 1981, and is made from spruce and maple. It has an exceptionally deep body and a bridge that shortens the length of the 5th and 6th strings. The resultant slight increase in tension improves the strings' "feel" and response.

John Buscarino, whose archtop guitars were featured on pages 76-77, offers a number of his models in a unique, "hybrid" form – with an archtop-style carved back and cutaway, but a round-hole, flat-top plate instead of an arched one with f-holes. The model illustrated is a 17-inch "Virtuoso;" Buscarino

also makes the instrument in a 16in (40.6cm) body width, and in a range of different finishes.

Jean Larrivée, in contrast to D'Aquisto and Buscarino, is a specialist in more traditional flat-top design. A Canadian whose instruments have a worldwide reputation, he has recently celebrated 30 years as a luthier. He started out as a maker of nylon-strung classical guitars, but began to build flat-tops in the early 1970s, in response to the folk music boom then sweeping Canada. Since then, his company has produced over 20,000 instruments; the Larrivée factory in Vancouver, British Columbia, uses some of the same computer technologies as Taylor Guitars, and Bob Taylor describes Jean as "one of my best guitar-building buddies." The beautiful headstock inlays found on many Larrivées are created by Jean's wife, Wendy. The model shown here features a mother of pearl, abalone and silver "Mucha Lady;" other instruments are decorated with dragons, jesters, angels, and djinns.

Below: D'Aquisto "Forté," 1981. The top is made from Tyrolean spruce, and the back and sides from German maple. The bindings and inlays are plastic, and the headstock features D'Aquisto's characteristic cut-out and finial.

(COURTESY JOHN MONTELEONE)

Right: Larrivée OM-10. It has a spruce top, a mahogany neck, and an ebony fingerboard.

Far right: The "Mucha Lady" on the headstock is made from mother-of-pearl, abalone, and ivoroid.

(COURTESY MANDOLIN BROTHERS, NEW YORK)

Top and opposite page, inset:
John Buscarino "Virtuoso" flat-top. The top is spruce; the back is carved from flamed maple.
(COURTESY JOHN BUSCARINO)

American and Canadian Flat-tops

Bill Collings, whose D3 flat-top is illustrated, makes his guitars in Austin, Texas. He began his career in another Texan city, Houston, working as a instrument repairman while establishing himself as a luthier in the mid-1970s. During this period, he made contact with a number of leading musicians on the local scene, including singer-songwriter Lyle Lovett, and his reputation spread rapidly. Collings moved to Austin in 1980, and in 1988 he received a major commission from fretted-instrument dealer and expert George Gruhn – an order for 24 guitars to be sold in Gruhn's Nashville music store. Collings guitars are now available worldwide; they are sought after by a wide range of players, and the larger-bodied models are especially popular with bluegrass performers. The D3 is Collings' top-of-the-line Dreadnought: this instrument, made in 1991, has sides and back of Brazilian rosewood (the traditional material of choice for flat-tops and classical guitars, now in very short supply due to deforestation).

William "Grit" Laskin is a Canadian luthier who is also a successful performer and songwriter; his songs have been recorded by Pete Seeger, the Tannahill Weavers, and other leading folk artists. Laskin's superb flat-tops often feature elaborate inlays, like the ones on this "Grand Auditorium" custom cutaway guitar, made in 1991. The stylized scene on the headstock and fingerboard, showing a trapeze with two acrobats and a crescent moon, includes a subtle visual joke: the seam of the female acrobat's leotard is positioned close to the tuning machine for the instrument's G string!

The third guitar shown is a Froggy Bottom model H, made in Newfane, Vermont by Michael Millard and his colleague Andrew Mueller. Millard has been building guitars for more than 27 years; the Froggy Bottom range includes everything from small-bodied instruments to Jumbos, Dreadnoughts, and twelve-strings. Among the leading names who play these guitars are singer-songwriter Dar Williams, and Will Ackerman, the co-founder of Windham Hill Records.

Above and below: *Laskin "Grand Auditorium" custom cutaway (1991). The term Grand Auditorium is used to describe medium-sized guitars, larger than OMs (Orchestra Models) but slightly smaller than Dreadnoughts or Jumbos.*
(Courtesy Mandolin Brothers, New York)

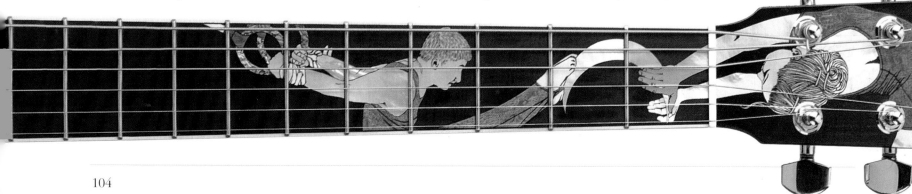

Left: *Froggy Bottom Model H. A "Grand Concert"-size guitar similar in dimensions to a Martin-style OM, and especially suited to ragtime and other fingerstyle playing. Froggy Bottom also make larger Dreadnought and Jumbo designs.*
(COURTESY MCCABE'S, SANTA MONICA)

Bottom of page: *Collings D3, c.1991. A Dreadnought design with a spruce top, rosewood back and sides, and abalone soundhole inlay. The bridge pins and nut are made from fossilized ivory.*
(COURTESY DALE RABINER)

Three American Luthiers

James Goodall, whose twelve-string Rosewood Standard is shown below, is a self-taught luthier who grew up in California. A former seascape artist, he built his first guitar in 1972, bartering one of his paintings to acquire the wood he needed. (Coincidentally, his source for supplies was the shop in Lemon Grove, California later acquired by Bob Taylor and Kurt Listug of Taylor Guitars.)

That instrument took him more than three months to complete, using tools borrowed from his father. Over the next few years, Goodall painstakingly acquired further knowledge and expertise, and in 1978, he became a full-time guitar-maker. Since 1992, he has been based in Kailua-Koni, Hawaii, where he currently produces about five instruments per week with the help of a small team of skilled employees.

James Goodall's mother was an art teacher in Southern California; one of her pupils, a teenager called Larry Breedlove, subsequently became production manager at Taylor Guitars.

Larry Breedlove and another Taylor employee, Steve Henderson, soon became close friends; in 1990,

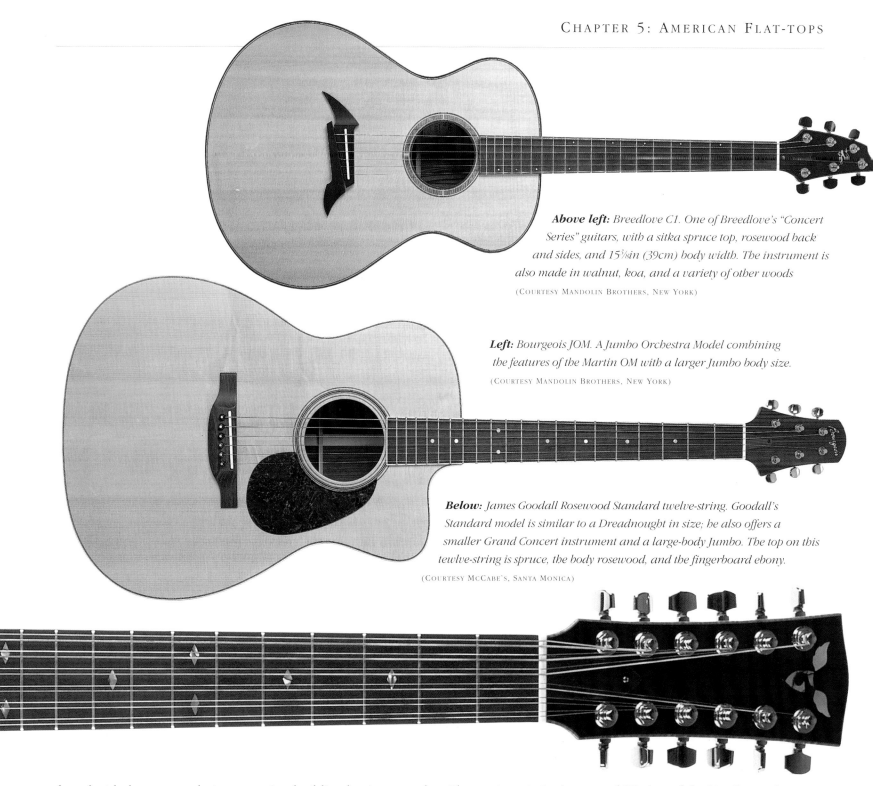

*Above left: Breedlove C1. One of Breedlove's "Concert
Series" guitars, with a sitka spruce top, rosewood back
and sides, and 15⅜in (39cm) body width. The instrument is
also made in walnut, koa, and a variety of other woods*
(COURTESY MANDOLIN BROTHERS, NEW YORK)

*Left: Bourgeois J.O.M. A Jumbo Orchestra Model combining
the features of the Martin OM with a larger Jumbo body size.*
(COURTESY MANDOLIN BROTHERS, NEW YORK)

*Below: James Goodall Rosewood Standard twelve-string. Goodall's
Standard model is similar to a Dreadnought in size; he also offers a
smaller Grand Concert instrument and a large-body Jumbo. The top on this
tewlve-string is spruce, the body rosewood, and the fingerboard ebony.*
(COURTESY McCABE'S, SANTA MONICA)

they decided to set up their own guitar-building business, and
the Breedlove Guitar Company was born. The company's
headquarters is just outside Bend, in the mountains of central
Oregon, and since 1994 (when Breedlove left the firm), Steve
Henderson has been in charge of instrument production
there. Breedlove guitars are immediately recognizable, with
their distinctively shaped headstocks and bridges, tight waists,
and smaller-than-average soundholes. The company makes
approximately 12 instruments per week, and in 1995 its CM
"Asymmetrical Concert" model won the American Guitar

Players Association's coveted "Guitar of the Year" award.

Dana Bourgeois, who collaborated with Eric Schoenberg
on the "Soloist" guitar (see pages 98-99), now runs his own
guitar-making company, based in Lewiston, Maine. He has over
20 years' experience as a builder and restorer, and is also a
highly respected teacher and writer on guitar design and
construction. Players of his instruments include country and
bluegrass star Ricky Skaggs and leading British folk guitarist
Martin Simpson. The Bourgeois model shown here is a Jumbo
OM – a modern adaptation of Martin's classic OM design.

CHAPTER 6
THE GYPSY GUITAR

While leading American luthiers were developing their archtop and flat-top guitars during the pre-World War II years, a visionary European musician and designer was following a slightly different path. Mario Maccaferri (1900–1993) was born in Bologna, Italy, and made his early reputation as a virtuoso classical guitarist. He was also a skilled luthier, and in 1930 he accepted an invitation to collaborate with the Paris-based Selmer company on a range of new guitar models bearing his name. Selmer insisted that one of these should be a steel-strung instrument aimed at jazz players, and Maccaferri, who was unfamiliar with jazz, decided to visit a night club to hear some. His impressions of the music were not very favorable, but he quickly

concluded that the most important factor in jazz guitar design was the need for a powerful, cutting tone. He achieved this on the Selmer-Maccaferri by using a slightly bent top to boost the sound (an idea borrowed from mandolin construction). The instrument also featured a distinctive D-shaped soundhole (changed on later models to an oval), and, on some early Maccaferris, a wooden resonator fitted inside the body.

The guitar, when it appeared, was highly successful throughout Europe, and became closely identified with the brilliant gypsy musician Django Reinhardt (1910–1953), whose recordings and performances as a soloist and with the Quintet of the Hot Club of France played a key influence in the development of the jazz guitar. Despite the success of his

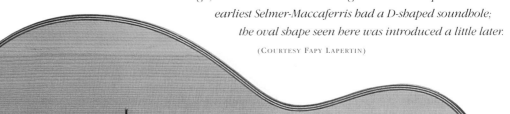

Below: *Selmer-Maccaferri, early 1930s. This is a superb example of an original Selmer-Maccaferri, still used regularly for concerts by its owner, the leading gypsy jazz player Fapy Lapertin. The slotted headstock and horizontally mounted tuning machines are characteristic features of this design, as are the "mustache" bridge and brass tailpiece. The earliest Selmer-Maccaferris had a D-shaped soundhole; the oval shape seen here was introduced a little later.*

(COURTESY FAPY LAPERTIN)

Left and far left: *D. J. Hodson Model 503 SRD. A replica of a D-hole Selmer-Maccaferri, made by a specialist UK luthier. The top of the instrument is spruce, its sides and back rosewood (the same woods were used on the original models). Hodson's logo, seen on the headstock, is modeled on Selmer's own trademark.*

(COURTESY CHARLES ALEXANDER)

Above: *Dupont Selmer-Maccaferri replica, c.1990. Maurice Dupont is one of the most distinguished contemporary European makers of Maccaferri-style instruments. Apart from the lighter color of the top, and the increased distance between the edge of the fingerboard and the soundhole, there is little to distinguish this guitar from the original on which it is modeled.*

(COURTESY DAVE KELBIE)

instrument, however, Mario Maccaferri's relationship with Selmer proved to be short-lived; he severed his relationship with the company in 1933 after a disagreement, and eventually left France to settle in the USA.

Selmer continued to manufacture Maccaferri's designs until the early 1950s; and since then several other guitar-makers have created replicas and re-interpretations of his instruments. Among them are the leading French luthiers Maurice Dupont and Favino, and a British craftsman, D.J. Hodson of Loughborough, Leicestershire, who was recently commissioned to build a 7/8th size instrument for Django Reinhardt's grandson, David.

Maccaferri and Monteleone

After emigrating to America in 1939, Mario Maccaferri became involved in a wide range of design projects, working on the production of violins, saxophone reeds, guitars, and ukuleles, all made from plastic. He also remained active in more traditional methods of instrument building, and developed a close relationship with one of today's leading American luthiers, John Monteleone, who recalls him as "a beautiful, incredible man. When I went up to his place, we'd sit down with his wife, Maria, have lunch together and tell stories, and then Mario would pick up the guitar after coffee and play for half an hour – beautiful classical arrangements. I was very fortunate to have had the opportunity to be a friend of his, and learn how to make a Maccaferri from Maccaferri himself."

During one visit to the Maccaferris, John Monteleone discovered a badly damaged Selmer-Maccaferri that had been given by Django Reinhardt's widow to the great American guitarist Les Paul. John successfully restored it, and went on to work with Mario on a number of instruments, including the "Django" model shown here. This experience led to the creation of his "Hot Club" model, which combines the Maccaferri-Selmer influence with John's own approach to body design. Unlike the original "bent-top" Selmers, the "Hot Club" has a flat top, and the oval soundhole is enlarged and reshaped to boost the bass and projection. On later versions of the guitar, the hole has been repositioned at a diagonal, and is higher on the left-hand bass side – a modification that further improves the instrument's treble and bass response.

Another departure from tradition on this and many other Monteleone guitars is the use of butcher bone instead of ivory for the nut and saddle. As John explains, he entrusts this material to an assistant: his dog, Sasha. "My dog is actually a participant – she is a luthier apprentice, and she has the benefit of preparation of the bone!"

Right and above, inset: *Monteleone Hot Club, 1993. John Monteleone's modern reworking of the Selmer-Maccaferri . Unlike the original models, this guitar has a flat top, and a fixed bridge is fitted instead of the "mustache"-style one. Maccaferri's oval soundhole has been replaced with an elliptical design that increases projection; it is edged with rosewood, which is also used for the back and sides. The top of the instrument is made from German spruce.*

(COURTESY JOHN MONTELEONE)

This page: Monteleone/Maccaferri Django, 1987. A collaboration between the leading American luthier John Monteleone – whose signature (inlaid in mother-of-pearl) can be seen at the twelfth fret on the fingerboard – and the then octogenarian Mario Maccaferri, who remained active as a designer until his death at the age of 93.
(COURTESY MANDOLIN BROTHERS, NEW YORK)

CHAPTER 7
THE RESONATOR GUITAR

$\mathcal{T}$he need to boost the acoustic guitar's relatively quiet sound has been addressed in many different ways by modern luthiers; but perhaps the most radical solution was devised by John Dopyera (1893–1988), who filed a patent in 1927 for a guitar fitted with three aluminum resonators, and went on to manufacture his invention through the National String Instrument Corporation.

John and his four brothers, Rudy, Louis, Emil (Ed) and Robert, were émigrés from Austro-Hungary who had settled in California with their parents. By the mid-1920s John and Rudy were running a thriving banjo manufacturing business in Los Angeles, and John had already developed a number of ingenious devices for improving the sound and playability of various stringed instruments. At around this time, a vaudeville singer and guitarist, George Beauchamp, approached the Dopyeras. Like many other players of the period, he was having difficulty being heard on stage, and he asked John to build him a Hawaiian guitar with a phonograph-style horn to increase its volume. The outcome of this idea, which had been inspired by the violin-with-horn designs previously developed by several other companies, was unsuccessful, and John Dopyera began to experiment with other methods of making Beauchamp's guitar louder.

He eventually came up with the resonator concept set out in his patent application. His prototype "tri-cone" guitar had a body not of wood, but "German silver" (an alloy of nickel, copper, and zinc). It was fitted with an aluminum, T-shaped bridge, topped with wood where the strings made contact with it, and mounted over a set of three aluminum diaphragms. The bridge carried vibrations from the strings to the three diaphragms, and the extra resonance they provided gave the instrument a powerful and distinctive tone.

Soon after John Dopyera filed his patent for the tri-cone, the new guitars went into production – first in John and Rudy's Los Angeles shop, and subsequently, on a larger scale, under the auspices of a company set up in 1928 by George Beauchamp and the Dopyeras: the National String Instrument Corporation. National had a revolutionary new product and an eager market for it – but before very long the new firm would be torn apart by bitter disagreements between its founders.

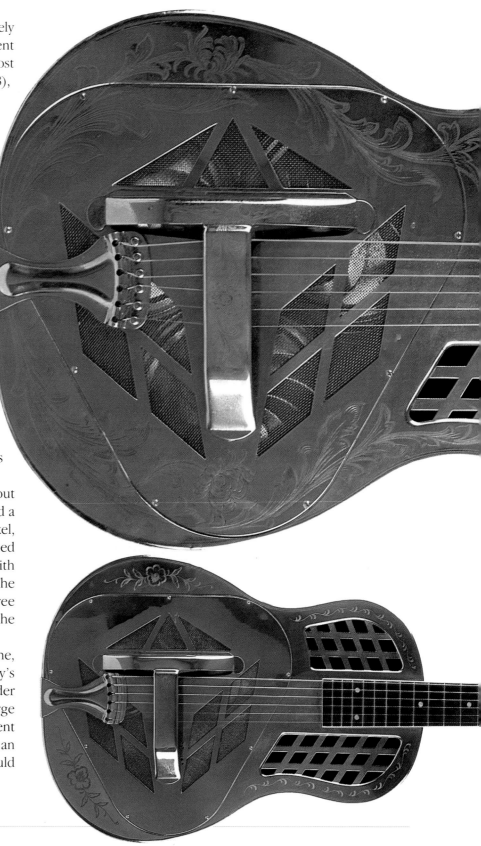

Below: *National Style 4 tri-cone, 1928. National's "top-of-the-line" Style 4 guitar was introduced in 1928 and remained in production until 1940. Its elaborate "chrysanthemum" engraving **(inset panel, below left)** was designed by George Beauchamp, the General Manager of the company. This is an early example of the model, which originally cost $195.*

(COURTESY MARK MAKIN)

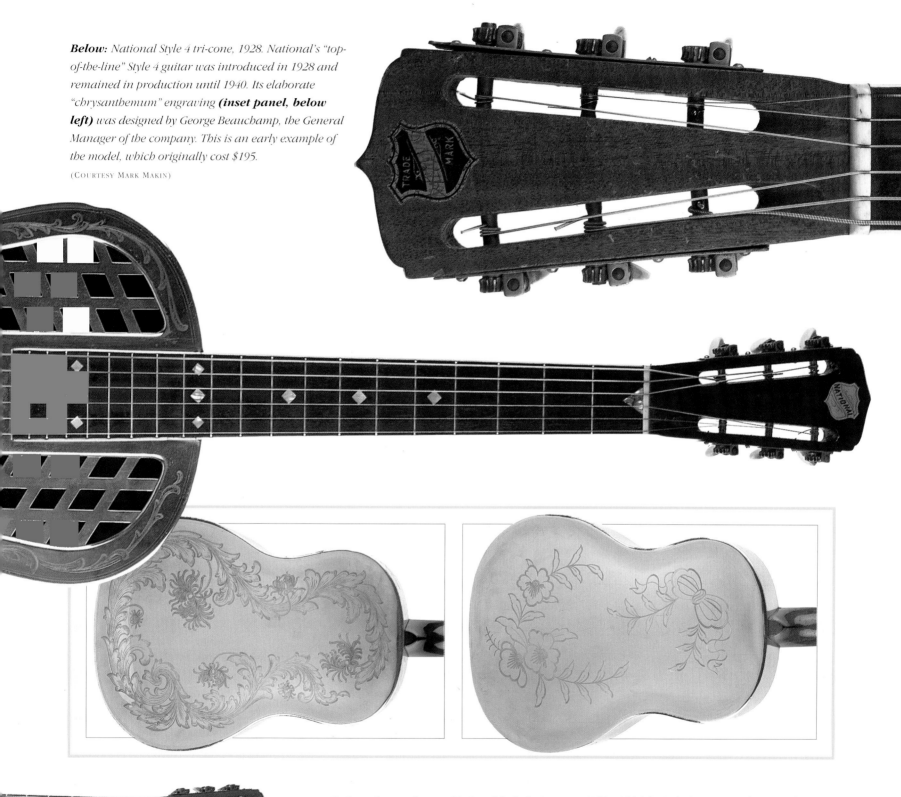

Left and top of page: *National Style 2 tri-cone, c.1929–1930. The Style 2 was one of National's most popular models; it was the cheapest of their resonator guitars to have a pattern engraved on it – a "wild rose" design **(inset panel, right)** created by Rudy Dopyera. This round-necked instrument is comparatively rare; most early National guitars were fitted with square necks for Hawaiian-style playing.*

(COURTESY MARK MAKIN)

National – The Early Years

*I*n 1928, National introduced another innovative guitar design, using just one aluminum resonator cone. This single diaphragm system was based on John Dopyera's ideas, but, in a move that infuriated Dopyera, George Beauchamp claimed the credit for it and eventually filed a patent for it under his own name. The ensuing row led to Dopyera's resignation from National in early 1929; later that year he formed the Dobro (Dopyera Brothers) Manufacturing Company, where he developed and marketed a rival single-cone resonator guitar.

This move led to deepening hostility with National. Beauchamp warned Dopyera's customers that the new Dobro guitar infringed National's patents, and Dobro reacted by bringing a $2,000,000 lawsuit against National. After a long and complex dispute, exacerbated by internal wrangles among National's directors, the case was settled out of court in 1933. The outcome was favorable to the Dopyeras; Beauchamp was ousted from the National board, and the two rival companies

formally merged in 1935. The following year, the National-Dobro Corporation moved to Chicago. It continued building its resonator instruments (including ukuleles and mandolins as well as guitars) until 1941, when the company was forced to cease production in the wake of the United States' entry into World War II.

In its relatively brief period of operation, the pre-War National Corporation made a bewilderingly large number of different models. The guitar range featured four-string tenor instruments, as well as Hawaiian and standard "Spanish" guitars, produced in a variety of decorative "styles." Some of these styles had names (e.g. "Duolian," "Triolian"), while others were simply known by numbers or letters (Style 1, Style 2, Style O, Style N, etc.) Many of these classifications were also used for National mandolins and ukuleles. The photographs here and on the previous pages show a cross-section of the designs produced by the company in the period between 1928 and the early 1940s.

Opposite page, left: *National Triolian wood-body single-resonator guitar, 1928. Not all Nationals were metal-bodied – the company made a variety of wooden instruments in the 1930s. This model, though, is a prototype; about 1,000-1,200 of them were produced between 1927–1928, mostly without serial numbers. Its design became the basis for the metal-bodied Triolian introduced in 1929. The plywood body and maple neck were constructed to be as dense and vibration-proof as possible. The colorful picture on the back (**opposite page, top left**) is screen-printed, and was probably applied via a water-slide transfer.*

(COURTESY MARK MAKIN)

Opposite page, center: *National Style 3 tri-cone, 1929–1930. A square-neck model for Hawaiian-style playing. Style 3 instruments featured a "lily-of-the-valley" engraving (**opposite page, top right**) designed by John Dopyera himself. They were made between 1928 and 1941.*

(COURTESY MARK MAKIN)

Opposite page, right: *National Style N single-resonator guitar, 1931. This brass-bodied model has a mahogany neck, ebony fingerboard, and pearloid-inlaid headstock (**left**), and is a more expensive version of the Style O, which featured a maple neck and fingerboard, and had no pearl finish. The instrument shown here has a 12-fret neck, but later Style Ns were built with a shortened body and 14-fret access.*

(COURTESY MARK MAKIN)

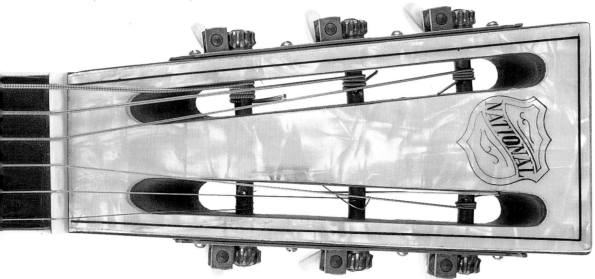

National Reso-Phonic Today

National never resumed production of metal-body resonator guitars after the War, but the Dopyera brothers revived the Dobro line in the 1950s, and eventually set up the O.M.I. (Original Musical Instrument) Company to manufacture Dobros in wood and metal. Among its employees in the early 1970s was Don Young, a luthier who had been fascinated by resonator guitars since childhood. Don subsequently left the company, gaining other experience in instrument building and repair, but returned in 1984 as plant supervisor. During his absence, he met McGregor Gaines, a graphic designer and skilled woodworker; they became friends, and McGregor soon joined Don at O.M.I., where he became shop foreman. The two craftsmen were keen to make improvements to guitar production; but in 1988, after several suggestions were rejected by the management, they resigned and began building National-type designs by themselves.

Below: National Reso-Phonic Style O single-resonator guitar. One of National's biggest-selling guitars, this is a recreation (with a striking new finish) of a design introduced in 1929. The body is made of nickel-plated brass.

(COURTESY NATIONAL RESO-PHONIC)

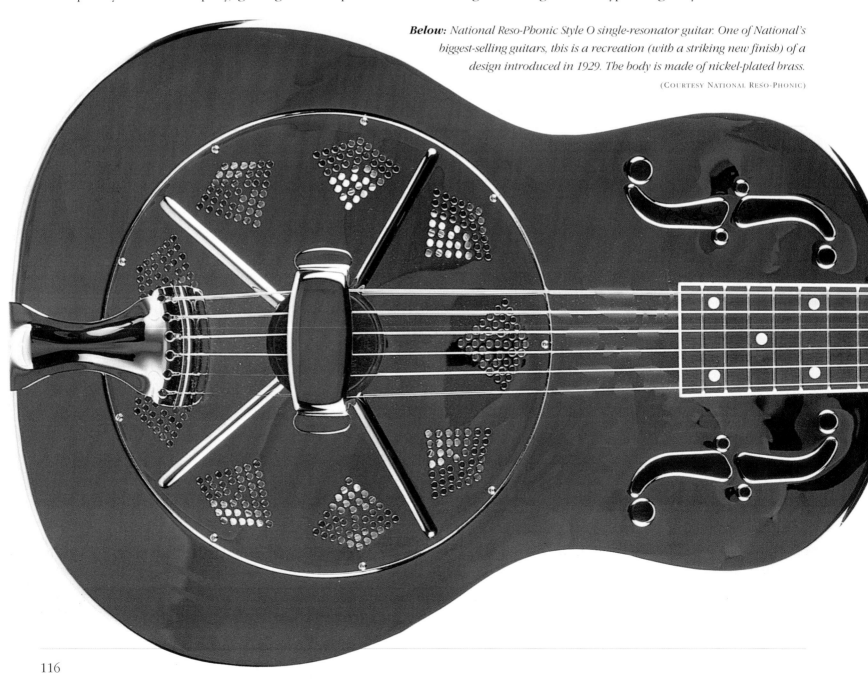

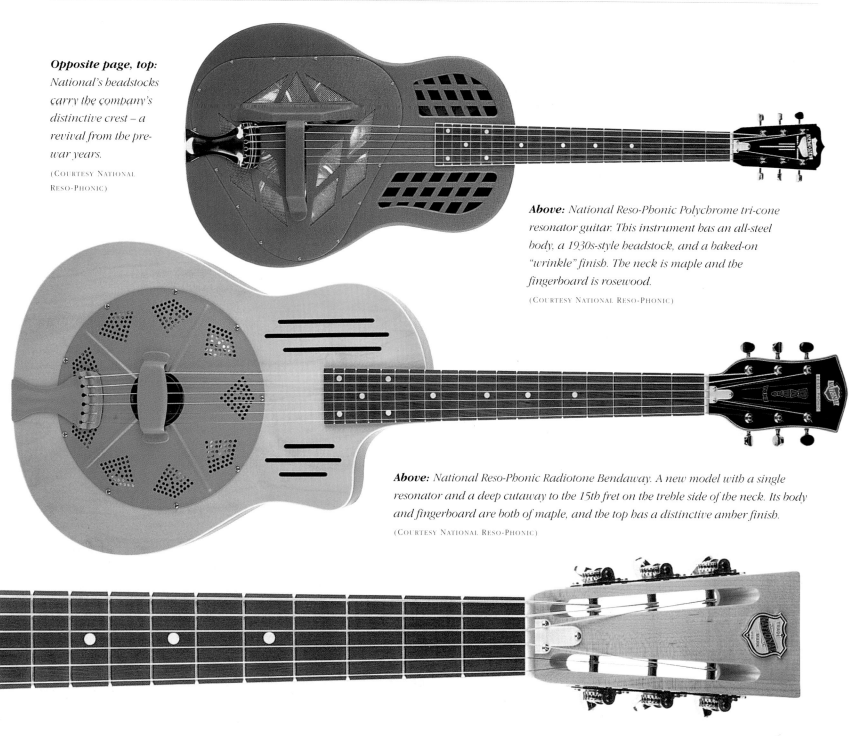

Opposite page, top:
National's headstocks carry the company's distinctive crest – a revival from the pre-war years.
(COURTESY NATIONAL RESO-PHONIC)

Above: *National Reso-Phonic Polychrome tri-cone resonator guitar. This instrument has an all-steel body, a 1930s-style headstock, and a baked-on "wrinkle" finish. The neck is maple and the fingerboard is rosewood.*
(COURTESY NATIONAL RESO-PHONIC)

Above: *National Reso-Phonic Radiotone Bendaway. A new model with a single resonator and a deep cutaway to the 15th fret on the treble side of the neck. Its body and fingerboard are both of maple, and the top has a distinctive amber finish.*
(COURTESY NATIONAL RESO-PHONIC)

For three years, Don and McGregor worked together to establish their new business, National Reso-Phonic Guitars, which is based in San Luis Obispo, about 200 miles (320km) north of Los Angeles. They built their first instruments in a garage, and were initially restricted to wooden models; the tooling for metal guitars was too expensive, and, as McGregor observes, "We were definitely lacking in capital. Good ideas don't impress banks!" However, the instruments Don and McGregor created found a ready market among National devotees, and by 1992 they were able to begin production of the two classic metal-bodied designs that are currently their biggest sellers: the Style O and the Delphi. National Reso-Phonic now employs 17 people, and makes 80 guitars a month. Don describes their instruments as "pretty close, structurally, look-wise and tonally, to the 1920s- and 1930s-type Nationals. We have definitely made some improvements, but that's not to snub the old stuff – our hats are always off to the old makers, and we're directly linked to the Dopyera brothers."

Recreation and Refinement

Don Young and McGregor Gaines had acquired a close knowledge of the Dopyera brothers' working techniques at O.M.I.; but they faced many difficulties in making National-style instruments for themselves. There were no written plans or blueprints for the original designs, and John Dopyera's patent applications, dating back to the 1920s, were not always a reliable guide to how the instruments had actually been produced. The only solution was to go back and examine the old guitars themselves: "We looked at them with a fine-tooth comb, studied the alloys, the resonators, the shapes, how they were put together." McGregor and Don quickly discovered that 1920s and 1930s Nationals had many design variations, even within production runs of the same model. When making their own versions of the instruments, McGregor explains that he and Don often had to "take a lot of different examples and try to work with the most graceful or most pleasing of the headstock styles or details."

The business of building Nationals for the 1990s involves both hand-crafting and high technology. Nearly all the company's necks – which used to take more than six hours to carve manually – are now made using high-precision Computer Numeric Control equipment. This completes the carving and fretting in only 12½ minutes, and can mill, slot and radius fretboards in seven minutes. Since acquiring CNC, National's production has increased by 80 percent. McGregor describes CNC as "a godsend – and it doesn't have mood swings or get cranky in the afternoon!"

Through their recreation of vintage National designs, and their development of exciting new acoustic and electric guitar designs, Don and McGregor have satisfied the demands of established resonator players, many of whom now play modern Nationals in preference to their fragile 1920s and 1930s instruments. And by raising the profile of the resonator guitar, the company is also helping to introduce it to younger performers, who, as Don Young observes, "are coming along, seeing this strange metal guitar with the hubcap on the front of it – and they go 'Wow!'"

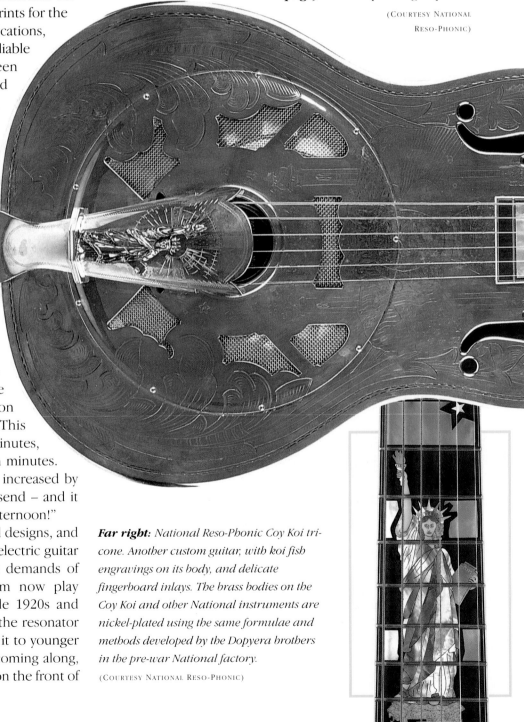

Below: National Reso-Phonic Liberty single-resonator guitar. This is a custom model showing off some spectacular mother-of-pearl headstock and fingerboard inlays. The figure of Liberty **(bottom of page)** on the tailpiece is gold-plated.

(COURTESY NATIONAL RESO-PHONIC)

Far right: National Reso-Phonic Coy Koi tri-cone. Another custom guitar, with koi fish engravings on its body, and delicate fingerboard inlays. The brass bodies on the Coy Koi and other National instruments are nickel-plated using the same formulae and methods developed by the Dopyera brothers in the pre-war National factory.

(COURTESY NATIONAL RESO-PHONIC)

Left: *National Reso-Phonic Estralita single-resonator guitar. A maple-bodied, walnut-colored version of a design first introduced by National in 1934. Its fingerboard is rosewood.*

*The headstock **(below)** is decorated with an ivoroid overlay and distinctive red lettering. The resonator cover-plate and tailpiece have a sleek, pewter-colored "baked-on" finish.*

(COURTESY NATIONAL RESO-PHONIC)

Right: *Headstock of the National Reso-Phonic Liberty guitar.*

(COURTESY NATIONAL RESO-PHONIC)

CHAPTER 8
THE TWENTIETH-CENTURY CLASSICAL GUITAR

Antonio de Torres had a profound influence on later guitar builders in Spain and beyond. His reputation spread rapidly, and the innovations he introduced became established practice for most of his successors. However, the next generation of great Spanish luthiers came not from the south of the country, where Torres lived and worked, but from the capital city of Madrid. It was here that José Ramírez (1858–1923), the founder of a long and distinguished family line of guitar builders, opened his instrument-making workshop in the early 1880s. Ramírez and his brother Manuel (1864–1916) – who was his first apprentice – became major figures in the development of Spanish lutherie, and were responsible for training a great many other famous craftsmen.

After collaborating for a number of years, the two brothers quarrelled bitterly over Manuel's decision to set up his own Madrid-based business in direct competition with José. The disagreement led to a permanent split, but even before this, significant differences were becoming apparent in the Ramírezs' guitar designs. While José frequently built thinner-bodied, harder-toned instruments that were especially popular with flamenco players, Manuel preferred the richer-sounding Torres style. His tastes are reflected in the work of his former apprentices, especially Domingo Esteso (1882–1937), who stayed with him for over 20 years, only setting up his own workshop after Manuel's death in 1916.

Another important Manuel Ramirez apprentice, Enrique García (1868–1922), subsequently moved east to Barcelona, where he established himself as a highly respected maker of guitars in the Torres tradition, winning a number of international awards for his instruments. His pupil, Francisco Simplicio (1874–1932), followed the same stylistic approach; the labels on his guitars proudly proclaim him to be "the sole disciple of Enrique García."

The third instrument shown here is by a maker from outside the "Madrid School" of luthiers, Salvador Ibanez, who had a workshop in Valencia during the early part of the twentieth century. It was used by the young Julian Bream in 1946 to give his first public recital in the English town of Cheltenham at the age of 13, and can now be seen in the musical instrument collection at Edinburgh University.

Below left: Guitar by Domingo Esteso, 1923. This instrument has a spruce top, Indian rosewood back and sides, and a rosette inlaid with an elaborate ring of mother-of-pearl on a black background.

(COURTESY GUITAR SALON INTERNATIONAL, SANTA MONICA)

Right: Guitar by Francisco Simplicio, built in 1929.

The absence of strings on the Simplicio guitar (it was undergoing repair when it was photographed) allows a clear view of the maker's label (above), which carries Simplicio's signature, and mentions the gold medal won by his teacher, Enrique García, at the Chicago Exhibition in 1893.

The Simplicio guitar is made from spruce and rosewood; its unusually tall and finely-shaped headstock (bottom right) is a characteristic of the luthier's work.

(COURTESY GARY SOUTHWELL)

Left: Guitar by Salvador Ibanez, early twentieth century. The top is made from pine wood, and the back and sides are of maple edged in ebony. Mahogany is used for the headstock and bridge, and the fingerboard is teak.

(COURTESY EDINBURGH UNIVERSITY)

The Flamenco Tradition

The rich sonorities of the post-Torres classical guitar were not ideally suited to all musical styles and techniques. In particular, flamenco performers, playing the fiery, often fiercely percussive gypsy songs and dances of Andalucía, sought a brighter, more cutting sound from their instruments. For them, Spanish luthiers evolved an alternative gut-strung guitar design, offering the hard brilliance of tone they desired.

Flamenco guitars are usually thinner and more lightly-built than their classical counterparts. Their bodies are frequently made from cypress, rather than the rosewood traditionally used for classical guitar backs and sides, and their tops are protected by *golpeadores* (tap plates) mounted on one or both sides of the soundhole, which perform a similar function to the pickguards on steel-strung guitars. Flamenco-style headstocks are also highly distinctive; they have no cut-

Below: Flamenco guitar by Manuel Ramírez, probably 1914. Like most flamenco instruments, this guitar has a cypress body; its top is pine, and it is fitted with simple friction pegs for tuning. (COURTESY EDINBURGH UNIVERSITY)

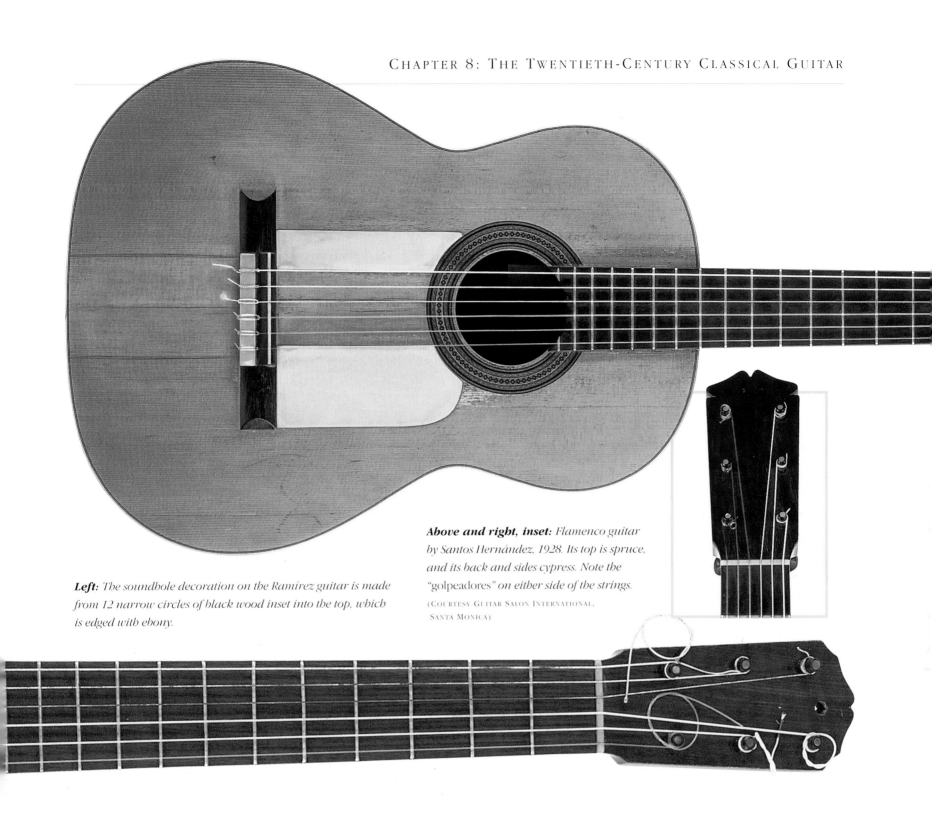

Left: *The soundhole decoration on the Ramírez guitar is made from 12 narrow circles of black wood inset into the top, which is edged with ebony.*

Above and right, inset: *Flamenco guitar by Santos Hernández, 1928. Its top is spruce, and its back and sides cypress. Note the "golpeadores" on either side of the strings.* (COURTESY GUITAR SALON INTERNATIONAL, SANTA MONICA)

outs or geared tuning machines, and are fitted with simple, vertically mounted wooden tuning pegs. Instruments of this kind were certainly available by the mid-nineteenth century; Torres himself made some of his less expensive models from cypress, and later designers gradually introduced other modifications. José Ramírez I was one of several Madrid-based luthiers who stiffened the tops of their guitars by arching them (another technique previously used by Torres), and many of his flamenco-style models also had enlarged bodies which provided increased volume. His brother Manuel took a

different approach; the guitar shown here, made by him in 1914, features a smaller body design and an unarched table.

Manuel Ramírez's flamenco designs were further developed by his former employee Santos Hernández (1874–1943), a distinguished luthier who also excelled at classical guitar construction. His designs have proved highly influential, and the important role he played in the early career of the great virtuoso Andrés Segovia, as well as the subsequent impact of his work on the leading German luthier Hermann Hauser, will be examined on the next two pages.

Andrés Segovia, Santos Hernández, and Hermann Hauser

Andrés Segovia (1893–1987) was soon to become internationally famous as the twentieth century's foremost classical guitarist; but in 1912, when he arrived in Madrid to make his concert début there, he was a relatively unknown 19-year-old without even an adequate instrument to use for the forthcoming recital. His search for a first-class guitar led him to Manuel Ramírez's workshop, where he made enquiries about hiring one. But having heard him play, Manuel is said to have been so impressed that he presented the young musician with a fine instrument that carried the Ramírez label, but was probably built by the luthier's foreman, Santos Hernández. Segovia used it not only for his Madrid performance, but also on many other worldwide concert engagements over the course of the next two decades.

Despite his esteem for the Ramírez/Hernández guitar, Segovia never commissioned another instrument from Santos Hernández himself. Instead, after discussions with several other craftsmen, he chose to collaborate with a leading

Below: *Guitar by Hermann Hauser, 1929. An instrument made during the period when Hauser was working with Andrés Segovia, perfecting the design for "the greatest guitar of our epoch."*

German luthier, Hermann Hauser (1882-1952), on the creation of what Segovia later described as "the greatest guitar of our epoch." While working on its construction, Hauser closely studied the Hernández as well as earlier Torres designs. After more than a decade of experimentation, he finally completed the instrument Segovia was seeking in 1936. It was used extensively by the great musician throughout the following 25 years, and can be heard on many of his finest recordings.

Hausers are among the most sought-after of all classical guitars; but the precise reason for what one leading dealer, Tim Miklaucic, describes as their "intangible, clear, and lyrical quality" is harder to determine. Gary Southwell, a luthier who has recently built a series of Hauser replicas for the great English guitarist Julian Bream, suggests that the secret may lie in the "sympathetic tunings" of the instruments. The tops of Hauser guitars have a resonant frequency of F# or G#, while the backs are pitched a tone lower, at E or F#; and when Gary built a replica that incorporated these tunings, Bream confirmed that he had come close to attaining the sound of the Hauser original.

Left: *After Hauser's death in 1952, his son continued to make instruments to a similar design as the 1929 model, and the luthier's grandson, Hermann Hauser III, is now custodian of the family tradition.*

(COURTESY GUITAR SALON INTERNATIONAL, SANTA MONICA)

Top right and right: *Guitar by Hermann Hauser, 1936. This guitar is known to have been owned and played by Segovia himself. It was subsequently taken to Latin America by the Uruguayan guitarist Abel Carlevaro, and during the 1950s it was repolished – probably in Hauser's own workshop. Since then, the wood on the body has shrunk slightly, leaving some fine lines visible on the finish.*

(COURTESY GUITAR SALON INTERNATIONAL, SANTA MONICA)

Segovia, José Ramírez III, and Ignacio Fleta

For much of the latter part of his career, Segovia played instruments by two Spanish luthiers, José Ramírez III (1922–1995, the grandson of José Ramírez I) and Ignacio Fleta (1897–1977). Ramírez's first assignment for Segovia was the repair of the maestro's treasured 1936 Hauser. He then began the lengthy process of developing his own designs to Segovia's satisfaction; his patience was rewarded in the early 1960s, when the guitarist started using Ramírez instruments regularly.

Ramírez made some significant departures from accepted tradition in his use of materials, preferring red cedar to spruce for the tops of his guitars, extending the string length of his instruments for extra projection and power, and creating special lacquer finishes to enrich their sound. Earlier, interest in exploring the acoustical principles underlying the art of instrument-making had been a source of friction with his father, José Ramírez II (1885–1957), another fine but more conservative

luthier, who felt that his son's researches were a waste of valuable time. However, José III's innovations – which also included the development of an efficient method of guitar production that enabled his craftsmen to turn out thousands of Ramírez instruments without sacrificing quality – have ensured him an important place in classical guitar history.

Ignacio Fleta was born at Huesa del Común, in the north-eastern Spanish region of Catalonia, in 1897. Trained as a violin and cello builder as well as a luthier, he made a variety of stringed instruments throughout the earlier part of his career, only focusing full-time on the guitar in 1955, after having heard a radio broadcast of Andrés Segovia playing a Bach transcription. Segovia was the first major player to use a Fleta (he acquired one in 1957, and subsequently bought two others), and since then, many other distinguished players, most notably John Williams, have been associated with his instruments. Fleta's two sons, Francisco and Gabriel, became partners in his Barcelona-based business during the 1960s, and they continued building guitars using the "Ignacio Fleta e hijos" ("and sons") label after their father's death in 1977.

Left: *Guitar by Ignacio Fleta, 1958. At this stage, Fleta was still using spruce for the tops of his guitars; he later changed to red cedar, as did José Ramírez III, the other luthier favored by Andrés Segovia during the last 30 years of his career. The instrument's headstock* **(opposite page)** *is based on the shape originated by Torres.* (COURTESY RAY URSELL)

Left, inset: *The Ignacio Fleta, 1958. Its label, bearing Fleta's name, shows the serial number of the instrument (No. 129).*

Right and far right: *Guitar by Ignacio Fleta, 1960. Another Fleta from the same period, also with a spruce top and rosewood back and sides. The neck and the headstock (which is veneered with rosewood) are cedar; and the fingerboard is ebony. The instrument retains its original French polish finish.*

(COURTESY SHEL URLIK)

Left: *Guitar by José Ramírez III, 1979. This is Ramírez's "Centanario No. 2" model, with a spruce top and Brazilian rosewood back and sides. The neck is cedar; the headstock is overlaid with rosewood and inlaid with real ivory.*

(COURTESY MANDOLIN BROTHERS, NEW YORK)

American Classical Guitar Makers

For many years, the main source for high-quality classical guitars was the instrument's birthplace – Spain. More recently, though, Spanish luthiers have faced growing competition from elsewhere in Europe, Japan, Australia, and, increasingly, the USA. American makers are now becoming as highly regarded for their classical designs as they have always been for archtops and flat-tops, and on these pages, we focus on three leading US luthiers whose guitars have achieved the acclaim of players and experts throughout the world.

Thomas Humphrey was born in Minnesota in 1948, but now lives and works in New York. He began his career there during the early 1970s in the workshop of Michael Gurian (a gifted luthier who was also associated with Michael Millard, the founder of Froggy Bottom Guitars – see pages 104-105), and started producing his own distinctive designs in the early 1980s. The most famous of these is the "Millennium," introduced in 1985, which features an unconventionally braced and steeply angled top. This is intended to increase the power of the instrument, while also improving access to the upper positions on the fingerboard. Humphrey's somewhat controversial designs are favored by leading guitarists such as Sharon Isbin, Carlos Barbosa-Lima, and Eliot Fisk; in 1997 he began a joint venture with the Martin Guitar Company to produce two classical models that will be built to his specifications.

Robert Ruck (b. 1945) is based in Hansville, Washington. A largely self-taught luthier, he produces approximately 30 instruments a year. He currently offers three basic sizes of guitar, which can be made as either "Standard" or "SP" (special, limited production) models. Robert Ruck guitars are used by a number of distinguished players, including the Cuban virtuoso Manuel Barrueco; he also builds a variety of other stringed instruments.

José Oribe (b. 1932) started making classical guitars in 1962 after earlier experience as an industrial machinist. Since 1973, his workshop has been in Vista, California. He offers his instruments in a variety of materials and finishes, laying great importance on the quality and seasoning of his tonewoods, all of which are aged for between 20 and 30 years before being used. Musicians playing Oribe guitars include fingerstyle jazz player Earl Klugh, and Angel and Pepe Romero.

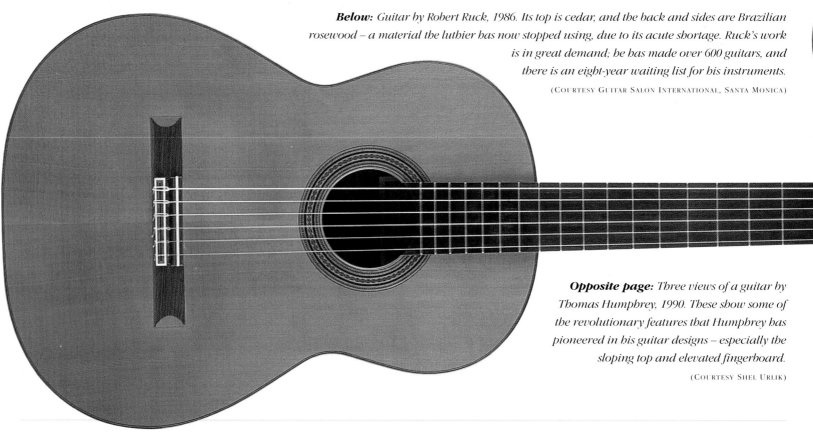

Below: Guitar by Robert Ruck, 1986. Its top is cedar, and the back and sides are Brazilian rosewood – a material the luthier has now stopped using, due to its acute shortage. Ruck's work is in great demand; he has made over 600 guitars, and there is an eight-year waiting list for his instruments.

(COURTESY GUITAR SALON INTERNATIONAL, SANTA MONICA)

Opposite page: Three views of a guitar by Thomas Humphrey, 1990. These show some of the revolutionary features that Humphrey has pioneered in his guitar designs – especially the sloping top and elevated fingerboard.

(COURTESY SHEL URLIK)

Left: *Guitar by José Oribe, 1982. This guitar features the same tonewoods as the Robert Ruck instrument. It is built in the style of José Ramírez III, whose work has been a major influence on Oribe.*
(COURTESY GUITAR SALON INTERNATIONAL, SANTA MONICA)

Left: *Thomas Humphrey uses an unconventional bracing system for the tops of his "Millennium" models, including an X-brace above the soundhole.*
(COURTESY SHEL URLIK)

Three British Luthiers

Probably the most internationally famous of UK-based classical guitar makers is David Rubio (b. 1934), whose Spanish-sounding name can be misleading. He was born David Spink, and re-named himself (taking his new surname from a village in Spain) while studying and performing flamenco as a young man. Fascinated by this music and by all things Spanish, Rubio spent a number of years during the late 1950s at the workshops of leading luthiers in Seville and Madrid. After learning the principles of guitar building from them, he moved to New York in 1961, eventually setting up a lutherie business of his own in Greenwich Village. Rubio returned to Britain in 1967, and for the next two years he worked closely with the great English guitarist and lutenist Julian Bream, designing instruments for him and other leading players.

During the 1970s, David Rubio became involved with designing and constructing a variety of other stringed instruments, but is now focusing on the guitar once again. The example of his work shown below dates from 1969.

Philip Woodfield lives and works in rural Cornwall, an area of England that holds a particular attraction for luthiers; the biographer of Torres, José Romanillos, once described it jokingly as "the graveyard for guitar-makers." Woodfield, however, is prospering there, and has produced over 130 instruments to date, including lutes, violins, and vihuelas as well as guitars. His designs are strongly influenced by Torres, and he prefers to work using traditional methods, avoiding the use of technology wherever possible. He has recently sold guitars to players throughout Europe, Japan, and the USA.

James Baker is a former student of Michael Gee at the London College of Furniture, which offers one of the UK's most highly regarded training courses for budding luthiers. He has now established a workshop in Suffolk, and Baker's instruments, like Philip Woodfield's, are in growing international demand.

Left: Guitar by David Rubio, 1969. It was made soon after Rubio's move from his workshop close to Julian Bream's home in Semley, Dorset, to new premises in the village of Duns Tew, Oxfordshire. David Rubio is now based in Cambridge.

(COURTESY RAY URSELL)

Left: Guitar by Philip Woodfield. This instrument is built in the Torres style, with a spruce top, and back and sides of Indian rosewood. Unlike some modern luthiers, Woodfield prefers to finish his instruments with a coating of shellac (which was also used by Torres) rather than varnish or lacquer; he has found that it improves the tone noticeably.

Although he sets great store by tradition, Philip Woodfield is also keen to experiment with new ideas – like the unusually carved and inlaid headstock **(below right)** on this guitar.
(COURTESY RAY URSELL)

Below left and right: Guitar by James Baker. The top is spruce, the back and sides are Brazilian rosewood, and the headstock is faced with bird's-eye maple.
(COURTESY RAY URSELL)

SECTION THREE
Today and Tomorrow

In the early 1960s, a British recording company turned down the chance of signing the Beatles because they believed that "groups with guitars were on their way out." The instrument's death-knell has been sounded many times since then; but despite fluctuations of taste and fashion, the guitar – and especially the acoustic guitar, in all its forms – has never been healthier or more in demand than it is now.

One of the most important trends in current attitudes towards the instrument is the value placed on vintage designs. The most "collectible" of these are no longer simply tools of the performer's trade, but desirable possessions, commanding prices that would have astonished their original owners and makers. Purchasers include not only professional musicians, but serious amateurs, and even non-players who buy guitars as investments.

This reverence for tradition is also reflected in the output of many contemporary guitar-makers. Gibson's success with its relaunched flat-top range (see pages 134-135) is evidence of customers' appreciation for classic models and fine craftsmanship. Even the most radical departures from standard methods, such as Alan Timmins' use of carbon-fiber bodies for his resonator guitars, often go hand in hand with painstaking research and replication of earlier designs; while other present-day luthiers, including Gary Southwell (whose work is profiled on pages 144-145), draw more direct inspiration from the past as they build their new, innovative instruments.

In this section, we survey these and other recent developments in guitar-making, showing some of the ways in which today's luthiers are answering their customers' needs by creating instruments suitable for almost all playing environments – from stage and studio to the home and even the open road!

Lowden LSE 1 cutaway acoustic guitar. This instrument, made by luthier George Lowden, whose company is based in Newtonards, Northern Ireland, features a sitka spruce top and mahogany back and sides. It is fitted with a built-in pickup, making it easy to amplify onstage; the volume control for this can be seen on the guitar's left shoulder.

(COURTESY CHANDLER GUITARS, KEW)

CHAPTER 9
TOWARDS THE FUTURE

The town of Kalamazoo, Michigan, had been associated with Gibson guitars ever since Orville Gibson went into business there in the 1890s. But in 1974, the company moved its electric instrument making to a new factory in Nashville, Tennessee, and ten years later, when the production of Gibson acoustics was also transferred there, the Kalamazoo plant closed permanently.

Its shutdown was a sad footnote to a difficult chapter in the great guitar-maker's history. In the wake of its takeover by the Norlin company in 1969, some controversial changes had been made to production methods. These included the introduction of double X-bracing on Gibson flat-tops – which succeeded in making the instruments more resilient, but impaired their tone-quality. By the early 1980s, sales were suffering, and a radical shift in strategy was needed to put the company back on track. It came in 1985, when Gibson was sold to a new management team, who worked hard to restore the firm's fortunes. In 1987, Gibson acquired a former mandolin factory in Bozeman, Montana, and re-equipped it for acoustic guitar construction; since 1989, all Gibson flat-tops have been made there, while production of other instruments continues in Nashville.

The company's recent output, which includes new designs and "reissues" of classic models from the past, has been highly acclaimed by musicians and dealers. Staff at the new plant at Bozeman use a combination of craft skills and computer-controlled technology to produce their instruments, and there is also a busy Custom Shop, making special orders and limited editions. Perennial Gibson favorites, like the J-200 seen here, and the Nick Lucas model that was the company's first high-quality flat-top (see pages 86-87), are now being built with the care and attention to detail these fine designs deserve, and many players compare the Montana guitars favorably with their vintage originals.

Below: *Gibson SJ-200. A newly-made instrument from the Gibson factory at Bozeman, Montana, closely based on the traditional J-200 design, which was originally launched in the late 1930s. The top is sitka spruce, the back and sides flamed maple. The acoustics currently being produced at Bozeman are among the finest Gibson have ever built.*
(COURTESY HANK'S, LONDON)

Below and below right (headstock): *Gibson Everly. This guitar is based on the "Everly Brothers" Jumbo first introduced by Gibson in 1963, and later renamed the J-180. Don Everly was responsible for designing the instrument's distinctive double pickguards, which were also fitted to the customized J-200s used by the brothers before the launch of their own model.*

(COURTESY HANK'S, LONDON)

Above left: *Gibson CL-40 Artist. One of a range of new acoustic designs produced by Gibson since their move to Montana. The CL-40 has a spruce top, rosewood back and sides, and an ebony bridge and fingerboard.*

(COURTESY HANK'S, LONDON)

Modern British Flat-tops

For many years, top quality UK-made flat-tops were few and far between, and most serious British players would usually be seen with a Martin, a Gibson, or some other "high-end" American instrument. Thanks to the work of a handful of skilled and enterprising luthiers, this situation has changed. British designs are now competing with the finest US guitars, and a growing number of musicians, not just in the UK but throughout the world, are making them their first choice.

The English West Country is an important center for British guitar building, and the distinguished luthier Andy Manson has lived and worked in Devon for more than a decade. His instruments are used by many discerning musicians, including Jimmy Page of Led Zeppelin and Ian Anderson of Jethro Tull, and the Manson range features Dreadnought models (the Sandpiper and the Dove), a Jumbo design (the Heron), and a guitar based on the classic Martin OM shape, the Magpie. Two of Andy Manson's associates, Andy

Below: Manson Magpie custom seven-string. Mansons all feature German spruce tops and Indian rosewood backs and sides. The Magpie is one of the company's most popular models, and this customized version was made for British jazz guitarist Andy Robinson.

(COURTESY ANDY ROBINSON)

This Magpie includes a small magnetized pillar on its top, providing a safe place for the player to put his pick!

Left: *Lowden O-12. Lowden's O (Original) series guitars are its largest instruments, with a lower bout width of 16⁹/₁₆ in (41.8cm). The O-12 has a sitka spruce top, and mahogany sides, back, and binding. Like almost all Lowden models, it has a two-piece bridge saddle to improve intonation on the first and second strings.*
(COURTESY CHANDLER GUITARS, KEW)

Above: *Fylde Oberon. This is Fylde's best-selling Dreadnought-style design, made in Penrith, Cumbria. The company's other models include smaller-bodied guitars like the Ariel and Goodfellow, and a Maccaferri-style instrument, the Egyptian.*
(COURTESY HANK'S, LONDON)

Petherick and Simon Smidmore of Brook Guitars, now build most of his standard designs, allowing Andy himself to focus on the production of specialized and custom instruments.

George Lowden is another long-established name in British lutherie. His Ulster-based company produces four basic models (with a wide variety of optional features), as well as a number of "Premiere Range" instruments made to special order from exotic tonewoods such as koa, black cedar, and Brazilian rosewood. Lowdens are played by singer-songwriter Richard Thompson, French fingerstylist Pierre Bensusan, and other leading guitarists on both sides of the Atlantic.

In 1973, Roger Bucknall, a British luthier with extensive experience of small-scale instrument production, set up the Fylde company, whose guitars gained a high reputation among leading UK folk performers such as Martin Carthy. Since then, Fylde's distinctive designs, often named after characters in Shakespeare plays, have attained a much broader popularity. As well as Dreadnoughts and smaller-body six-strings, the company has also pioneered two successful acoustic bass guitars, the King John and the Sir Toby. Fylde's customers include Sting, Pat Metheny, Martin Simpson, and English actor/singer Jimmy Nail.

Ovation Guitars

Twentieth-century luthiers have introduced many major changes in guitar construction; but – with the notable exception of the Dopyera brothers and their "German silver" instruments – they have nearly all continued to use wood as the basis for their designs. Companies experimenting with other materials, particularly man-made ones, have often had to face considerable resistance and criticism; and so far, only one large-scale American manufacturer, Kaman, has succeeded in overcoming this by achieving mass-market success for its "Lyrachord"-backed Ovation guitars.

Kaman was originally an aerospace engineering company, although its Chairman, Charlie Kaman, has always been a keen guitarist. In 1964, he and a team of technicians began analyzing the ways in which various guitars absorbed and reflected sound. Having found that instruments with rounded backs were more acoustically efficient than traditional flat-back shapes, they used their discoveries to create a radical new design – and the outcome was the Ovation Balladeer, which appeared in 1969. It had a spruce top, but its novel "bowl-back" was manufactured from Lyrachord, a specially-developed fiber-glass formulation that is strong, sonically reflective, and impervious to climate change.

The company's earliest models were entirely acoustic; but in the early 1970s, it pioneered the development of high-quality, feedback-resistant piezo-electric pickup systems for its guitars, and as a result, Ovations became especially popular for stage work. Although opinion remains divided about the instruments' sound and shape, a number of eminent players use them regularly. These include Glen Campbell (Ovation's first and most influential endorsee), as well as solo guitarists Adrian Legg and Al Di Meola, singer-songwriter Joan Armatrading, and Latin jazzman Charlie Byrd (who plays a nylon-strung model).

Kaman has continued to experiment with other non-traditional materials, including graphite (which is used instead of wood for the top of its Adamas model); but only a handful of other companies and luthiers are currently working with synthetics. Among them is Alan Timmins, an English designer with a ground-breaking design for a carbon-fiber resonator guitar, whose highly distinctive work is featured on the following two pages.

Above: *Ovation Standard Balladeer. The Balladeer was the first model introduced by Ovation; this is the current version, with a spruce top, two-piece neck, and mahogany fingerboard, and the company's distinctive Lyrachord back. The guitar also has a built-in pickup and preamplifier.*
(COURTESY CHANDLER GUITARS, KEW)

Right: *Ovation Celebrity Deluxe. It is a shallower-backed Ovation model, fitted with an under-bridge pickup system. The cutaway fingerboard edge, characteristic "leaf" design, and holes on the upper top are also found on other Ovations, including their top-of-the-range Adamas guitar.*
(COURTESY CHANDLER GUITARS, KEW)

Below left: *Ovation Custom Legend. A "high-end" Ovation with a sitka spruce top, mahogany and maple five-piece neck, and abalone purfling and fingerboard position markers. The tuning machines are gold-plated, with pearloid buttons.*
(Courtesy Hank's, London)

Left: *The Lyrachord fiber-glass material used for the Balladeer and its distinctive shaping were by-products of Ovation founder Charlie Kaman's earlier work on helicopter design. He explained recently that "In helicopters, the engineers spend all their time trying to figure out how to remove vibration. To build a guitar you spend your time trying to figure out how to put vibration in. But vibration is vibration."*

Alan Timmins and his Resonator Guitars

Alan Timmins, from Nottingham, was almost certainly the first luthier in Britain to build resonator guitars. Since developing a metal-bodied tricone in 1989, he has gone on to create carbon-fiber models now used by Mike Cooper, Dave Peabody, Michael Messer, and other leading players. Alan's wide-ranging technical expertise has been an important factor in the success of his designs, as has the support of his friend Mark Makin – the UK's foremost authority on the history of National guitars, who lives nearby, and commissioned Alan's first instrument.

This was based on a National Style 97 (the design that replaced the company's Style 1 in the late 1930s), and was the first metal guitar Alan had ever made. He was soon working on other instruments: "I built half-a-dozen, maybe ten of them…but there were 16 bits of metal in each guitar, and it was a struggle, all the soldering, warping and lining up – a nightmare of a job." He decided to make molds, and use these to construct his guitar bodies from carbon fiber. This simplified the production process, which required only two moldings: one for the back and sides, and one for the front.

The outcome of Alan's experiments was his F1 model. The strength and durability of its body's carbon-fiber formulation provides remarkable

stability. Alan guarantees his instruments "airport baggage-handler-proof," and unlike metal-bodied guitars, they do not expand and go out of tune when exposed to heat. Wood is still used for the neck, and the cover-plates are made from laser-cut brass.

The crucial question of how the carbon-fiber bodies sound is best answered by one of Alan Timmins' customers, blues guitarist Dave Peabody, who summarized his reactions – and those of his audience – in a recent edition of *Blueprint* magazine. "Apart from looking wonderful, being black and silver, it's got *the tone* to me. It's very loud and it projects brilliantly into a microphone…I picked [my instrument] up on my way to the Edinburgh Blues Festival, where it had its inauguration. And it got a round of applause on its own."

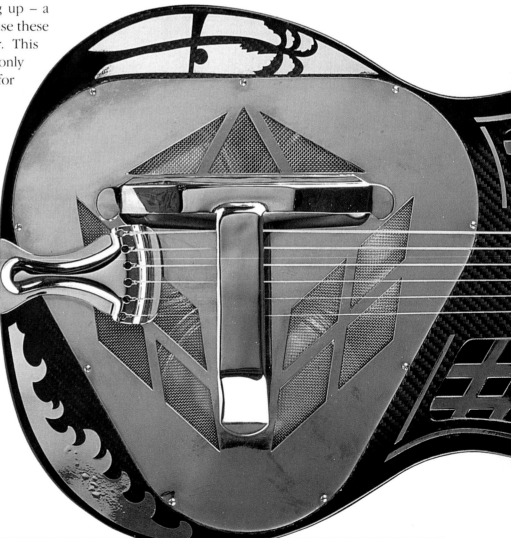

Left: *The bodies for Alan's carbon-fiber instruments are molded in two pieces (sides/back and front), and then left to cure for up to a fortnight. The National metal-bodied instruments on which the F1 is based were made from shiny metal, with matt decorative patterns sandblasted on. The F1* **(left)** *reverses this: the bodywork is matt, the design (another version of Alan's "surfer girl") shiny.*

Below left: *Alan Timmins Style 97-type tricone, 1989. This guitar, custom-built for Mark Makin, was one of the first to be made since National stopped producing the designs in the 1940s. The back* **(top left)** *features Alan's "surfer girl" and "palm-tree" decorations.*
(COURTESY MARK MAKIN)

Left and right: *Alan Timmins F1 carbon-fiber tricone. The guitars' necks are made either from mahogany or, as on this model, from laminated maple with an ebony strip. The headstock is carbon-fiber, and the "F1" inlay and fingerboard markers are abalone.*

(COURTESY ALAN TIMMINS)

Travel Guitars

Acoustic guitars can be demanding traveling companions. Their dimensions make them unsuitable as in-flight hand luggage, and many musicians are unhappy about exposing their delicate instruments to the rigors of aircraft holds and baggage carousels. Other means of transport can be equally hazardous; yet keen players hate to be parted from their guitars on holidays or business trips. Recently, several American companies have offered a solution to this dilemma by developing smaller instruments that retain the feel – and some of the sound – of full-size models. Three examples are shown here.

Right: *Baby Taylor. A highly acclaimed instrument designed by Bob Taylor and his team for travelers and younger players – although it has also proved very attractive to more experienced guitarists. It has a spruce top, a mahogany neck, and mahogany veneer back and sides. The soundhole decoration is created using a computer-controlled laser etching process, and the fingerboard and bridge are ebony.*

(COURTESY TAYLOR GUITARS)

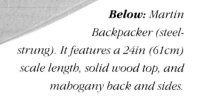

Below: *Martin Backpacker (steel-strung). It features a 24in (61cm) scale length, solid wood top, and mahogany back and sides.*

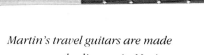

Martin's travel guitars are made under licence in Mexico.

(COURTESY MARTIN TAYLOR)

The Baby Taylor is a remarkable piece of design, offering a deep, Dreadnought-style body and a standard-width neck on an instrument that measures only 34in (86.4cm) from headstock to endpin. It has many of the features found on full-size Taylors, including an X-braced sitka spruce top and ebony fingerboard, and unlike some travel guitars, it is designed to be played at standard pitch. The Baby Taylor was introduced in 1996, and has proved popular not only with travelers and children, but with a number of leading professionals who have used it onstage and in the studio.

Martin's Backpacker has an unconventional look and feel. Its small, exceptionally light body is combined with a heavier, full-size neck, and a strap is needed to keep the instrument in the correct playing position. The guitar shown here is a steel-strung model; Martin also produces a nylon-strung Backpacker with a slightly wider and longer body. Both instruments can be amplified using built-in pickup systems. They provide excellent access to the upper positions on the fingerboard, and have a pleasing, slightly banjo-like sound.

Tacoma Guitars' P1 Papoose model is intended to be tuned a 4th higher than normal (i.e. the first string, normally E, becomes an A). It is fitted with a cedar top, featuring Tacoma's unusual low-mass triangular bracing system, and a mahogany back and sides. The Papoose has recently been endorsed by country music stars Vince Gill and Ricky Skaggs.

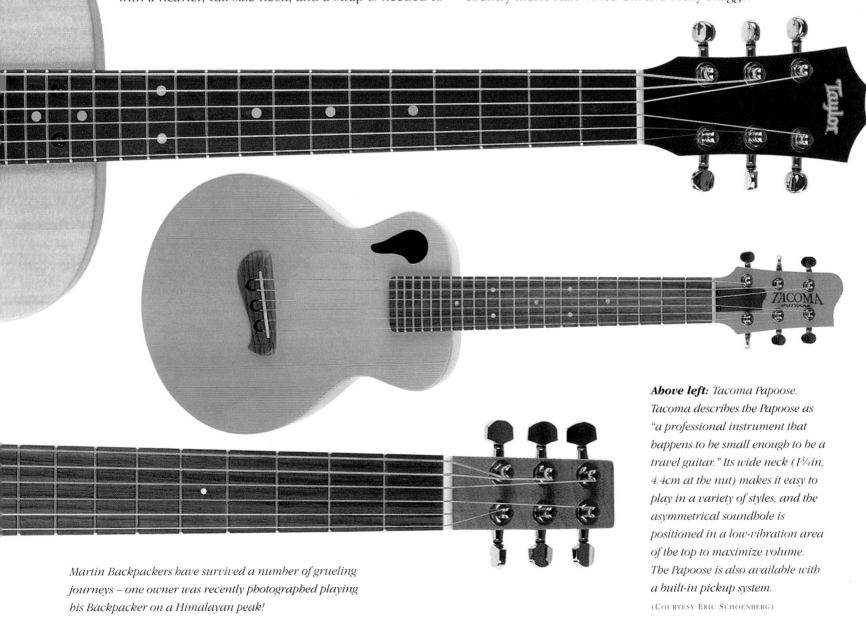

Martin Backpackers have survived a number of grueling journeys – one owner was recently photographed playing his Backpacker on a Himalayan peak!

Above left: *Tacoma Papoose. Tacoma describes the Papoose as "a professional instrument that happens to be small enough to be a travel guitar." Its wide neck (1¾in, 4.4cm at the nut) makes it easy to play in a variety of styles, and the asymmetrical soundhole is positioned in a low-vibration area of the top to maximize volume. The Papoose is also available with a built-in pickup system.*

(COURTESY ERIC SCHOENBERG)

Gary Southwell – Inspiration from the Past

ritish luthier Gary Southwell draws inspiration from a range of different classical guitar-making traditions. He has built Hauser replicas, as well as Torres-style instruments, and guitars based on earlier French and German models. Gary also creates his own strikingly original designs, which reflect his detailed knowledge of the past while offering ingenious new approaches and ideas.

Illustrated here is a Southwell replica of an instrument by the French luthier René Lacôte (1785–1855). Guitars from this period were smaller than the Torres designs that later became the accepted standard for makers and players; but their well-focused sound provides sufficient volume for many modern concert halls, as Gary explains. "Although they don't have the warmth and depth of a post-Torres guitar, they do have a very clear, ringing tone which tends to penetrate and cut through very well." The Lacôte replicas are used by a number of distinguished players, including early music expert Nigel North, and David Starobin, who has also worked closely with Gary on the development of his "Series A" range.

Gary describes the Series A designs as "my modern interpretation of the Viennese tradition of classical guitar making." The "A" stands for "adjustable," and the instruments feature a refined version of the moveable neck system invented by Johann Georg Stauffer (1778–1853) and used on early guitars by his pupil C.F. Martin. A key in the heel of the neck allows the string action to be raised or lowered swiftly, even in mid-concert; and the "floating" fingerboard is free from contact with the top, increasing the overall vibrating area. The instrument's shape follows French and Viennese tradition, with a more pronounced waist than later Spanish guitars; while the intricately inlaid rosette is based on a Neolithic rock carving seen by Gary in Northumberland.

Gary aims to provide musicians with instruments that are inspiring, practical, and versatile. As he says, "To me the most important thing about a guitar is that it responds to what the player wants to do to it. A lot of guitars dictate to the player, I want to make an instrument that's full of character, but has the ability to be directed and enjoyed by the player."

Below: Gary Southwell replica Lacôte guitar. Its top is spruce, and the back and sides birdseye maple – a wood commonly used in nineteenth-century French guitars like the one on which this instrument is based. The neck is made from an ebony veneer, with an ebony fingerboard, and the edgings are a combination of ebony and sycamore. (COURTESY GARY SOUTHWELL)

This page: *Gary Southwell Series A guitar.
Again, a spruce top is used, with Honduras
rosewood back and sides, a birdseye maple
neck, and ebony fingerboard. The
elaborate rosette is made from inlaid
bone and ebony tiles, with a "Neolithic"
design carved in. The removable key
in the heel of the neck controls a
mechanism allowing the height of the
strings to be adjusted by the player.*
(COURTESY GARY SOUTHWELL)

Martin Taylor and the Yamaha Electro-Acoustic

The defining line between "acoustic" and "electric" instruments is not easy to draw. Almost all steel-strung acoustic guitarists (and even a few of their classical colleagues) now use some form of amplification onstage, while a number of electric archtop players like to combine the signal from their magnetic pickups with natural, acoustic tones. When performing in a live, feedback-prone environment, this is often difficult to achieve – but one musician who can easily combine or alternate between the two sounds, thanks to the Yamaha guitar he helped to design, is distinguished British jazzman Martin Taylor.

In 1989, Yamaha approached Martin with an idea for a guitar with two pickups: a conventional humbucker in the neck position, and a piezo device to capture the acoustic sound. He worked on detailed plans for the instrument with Martyn Booth of Yamaha-Kemble U.K., and these were eventually submitted to the company's Design Department in Hamamatsu, Japan. There, luthier Jackie Minacuchi built a prototype, which Martin used on his "Artistry" CD (1992) and on subsequent tours. He then sent a list of suggested modifications back to Minacuchi, who responded with a second prototype; Martin has never used this for live dates or recordings, although he has frequently played it at home. After some further changes, Yamaha completed the final, production version of the design, the Martin Taylor AEX 1500; it can be seen opposite, together with the two prototypes.

The Yamaha is now Martin Taylor's main working instrument, providing him with the range of tone-colors he needs for both solo and group work. He has used it on many TV appearances, videos, and CDs, including the "Portraits" album, recorded in Nashville with veteran country music guitarist and producer Chet Atkins. During the sessions, Chet paid tribute to Martin by signing his guitar with the simple inscription: "Your the best" (sic).

Below: *Yamaha Martin Taylor AEX 1500 – production model. Martin Taylor uses this instrument as his main working guitar. It offers electric and acoustic sounds, with edge-mounted controls to mix and equalize them. Chet Atkins' signature and personal message to Martin* **(inset)** *are visible near the tailpiece.*

(COURTESY MARTIN TAYLOR)

Below: Yamaha Martin Taylor AEX 1500 – first prototype. One of only two initial prototypes of the guitar developed by Martin Taylor and Martyn Booth, and hand-built by luthier Jackie Minacuchi. Martin has toured and recorded widely with it.

This prototype AEX 1500 is owned by Martin Taylor himself; the other is kept at Yamaha's Design Department in Hamamatsu, Japan.

(COURTESY MARTIN TAYLOR)

Below left: Yamaha Martin Taylor AEX 1500 – second prototype. This guitar was made after Martin requested some alterations and improvements to prototype No. 1; again, only two identical examples of the revised design were ever built.

(COURTESY MARTIN TAYLOR)

The Contemporary Guitar

Since its emergence in the sixteenth century, the acoustic guitar has evolved into many differing forms, and this process continues today, as luthiers combine ideas and designs from various traditions to create new and exciting instruments. The three guitars shown here are all examples of this eclectic approach, and they form a fitting conclusion to this book.

Robert Benedetto's "Il Fiorentino" is a nylon-strung archtop guitar with strong echoes of classical violin design. The first model in Benedetto's "Renaissance" series, which also includes a similar steel-strung archtop, "Il Palissandro" (The Rosewood), its top is made from aged European spruce, and the back and sides from European curly maple, with a centerpiece of American birdseye maple. The instrument dates from 1994.

Paul McGill, a luthier based in Nashville, Tennessee, builds outstanding classical instruments as well as resonator guitars, and this colorful Dobro-type model, made by him in 1995, has a Spanish guitar-style headstock and fingerboard. The resonator cover is decorated with sapwood – the soft wood found directly underneath tree bark. Paul McGill's customers include Chet Atkins, Earl Klugh, Ricky Skaggs, Phil Keaggy, and many other leading names.

The final instrument brings together the traditions of jazz and classical guitar making. Its creator, John Buscarino, calls it the "Cabaret;" its body is based on the designs of the great German luthier Hermann Hauser, but its cutaway and built-in pickup make it especially suitable for fingerstyle jazz performers. One leading British jazz musician, Adrian Ingram, has described it as "the best amplified nylon-string guitar I have ever played."

Outstanding instruments like the ones seen here – and elsewhere in this book – are proof that acoustic guitar building is currently reaching new heights of excellence. As Don Young of National Reso-Phonic puts it: "People need to realize that right now the guitar industry as a whole, whether it's the individual luthier or some of the bigger companies, are making some of the best guitars that have ever been produced. We're in a very rich period, and I commend all our fellow guitar-makers out there for doing a fine job."

Right and above, inset: *Benedetto "Il Fiorentino" 16-inch archtop nylon-strung guitar, 1994. A radical departure from standard archtop design. It is built from European and American tonewoods, with a wood burl veneer on its classical guitar-style headstock. Solid ebony tuning pegs are used as opposed to conventional tuning machines. It features a violin-style bridge, hand-carved from curly maple, and an ebony tailpiece (with abalone inlay), which is attached to the body using cello tailgut.*

(COURTESY ROBERT BENEDETTO)

Left and far left: *Paul McGill resonator guitar. McGill's resonator designs are influenced by Dobros and by the now-rare Brazilian DelVecchio instruments favored by leading players such as Chet Atkins, who also owns a McGill resonator model like the one shown here. The neck and top are fashioned from cedar, the back and sides rosewood, and the fingerboard is made from ebony.*
(COURTESY MANDOLIN BROTHERS, NEW YORK)

Bottom of page: *Buscarino Cabaret cutaway. John Buscarino designed this instrument to provide "the perfect blend of a traditional classical guitar and an acoustic archtop guitar." He also makes a slightly larger "Grand Cabaret," based on a José Ramirez III model.*
(COURTESY JOHN BUSCARINO)

Glossary

acoustic guitar   Guitar capable of creating and projecting its sound without electronic assistance. While acoustic guitars are frequently amplified for stage use, their capacity for producing a usable sound by themselves differentiates them from *electric guitars*, which rely on pickups and amplification to be heard.

action   Height of *strings* above the guitar's *fingerboard*. A low action makes it easy for a player to form notes and chords with his/her fretting hand, but may compromise the instrument's tone and cause string buzzing. High action often improves and boosts the sound, but can lead to playing difficulties.

alfabeto   Early system of chord symbols for guitar, introduced in 1595 and used widely in published music throughout the seventeenth century (see page 16).

archtop guitar   Guitar (usually steel-strung) with *top* carved or pressed into an arched shape (cf *flat-top*).

binding, purfling   Strip(s) of wood, plastic, or other material decorating the edges of a guitar's body.

bourdon   Term used to describe the tuning of the *courses* on some early guitars, in which one of the two strings making up the course would play at a given pitch, while the other would provide a note that sounded an octave lower. Occasionally, the lower note would be omitted altogether (see *re-entrant tuning*).

bout   Most guitars have bodies shaped like a figure-of-eight; the wider sections above and below the *waist* are referred to as the upper and lower bouts. *Archtops* and *flat-tops* are frequently categorized by the maximum width of their lower bouts (17 inches/43.2cm, 18 inches/45.7cm, etc.)

bowl-back   Rounded back shape found on some early guitars, and also used on modern Ovation instruments (see *lyrachord*)

bridge   Unit mounted on the lower part of a guitar's *top*, and fitted with one or more *saddles* of bone, ivory, or synthetic material. It sets the end of the *strings'* vibrating length (which begins at the *nut*); as the strings pass across it, their vibrations are transferred to the *top*. It can also be adjusted to affect the strings' height and intonation. On *classical* and some *flat-top* guitars, the bridge provides an anchor for the string ends, which are passed through holes in its structure, and pinned or tied down. On *archtop* guitars, the strings are anchored by the *tailpiece*, and the bridge is usually a moveable assembly, held in place by string pressure.

bug   See *piezo-electric pickup*.

burl   Naturally-occuring knot in a piece of wood.

chitarra battente   Wire-strung guitar played with a *plectrum* and used for chordal accompaniment. The earliest known examples date from the seventeenth century.

classical guitar   Instrument modelled on the designs of Antonio de Torres (1817–1892) and his successors, with six gut (later nylon) *strings*. It is played *fingerstyle* with the nails or fingertips.

CNC   Computer Numeric Control. A method of controlling high-precision machine tools with computers during guitar manufacture.

course   Pair of *strings* tuned in unison or in octaves, and fretted and struck simultaneously.

cutaway   Incision in the upper part of the guitar body adjacent to the neck, allowing the player's fretting hand to reach the highest positions more easily.

Dobro   Type of *resonator guitar* first developed by the Dopyera brothers in the 1930s after their departure from the National String Instrument Corporation.

Dreadnought   Large-bodied, *flat-top acoustic guitar* design first introduced by the Martin company in the early 1930s, and named after a famous class of battleship. The Dreadnought style has been widely imitated by other guitar builders. See *Jumbo*.

electric guitar   Solid, semi-solid, or hollow-bodied steel-strung guitar fitted with one or more electro-magnetic pickups. These convert the vibrations of the strings to alternating current, which is fed to an amplifier, boosted, and projected to listeners via loudspeakers. Many electric guitars produce little or no direct acoustic sound, and are not designed for use without amplification – unlike *acoustic* or *electro-acoustic* guitars (qv).

electro-acoustic guitar   Acoustic guitar with built-in electro-magnetic and/or *piezo-electric pickup*(s); usable with or without amplification.

f-hole   *Soundhole* in the shape of an "f" or its reversed image, traditionally used on bowed string instruments. First adopted on *archtop guitars* by the Gibson company in 1922.

fan-bracing, fan-strutting   A series of thin wooden braces glued onto the underside of a *classical* or flamenco guitar *top* in a radiating fan pattern. Fan-bracing strengthens the top and controls its vibrations (see page 42).

fingerboard   The front surface of the guitar's neck, fitted with *frets*, and extending downwards from the *nut* towards the body and onto (or over) the instrument's *top*. Its surface or edge is often embellished with decorative position markers, which provide "landmarks" for the player's fretting hand.

fingerpicks   Plastic, metal, or tortoiseshell attachments, worn on the fingers and/or thumb of a steel-strung guitarist's striking hand, and used to increase the power and clarity of *fingerstyle* playing.

fingerstyle   Method of striking the guitar *strings* with the thumb, first, second, and third fingers, rather than with a *plectrum*. In modern *classical guitar* technique, the fingernails are used; this method was favored by some nineteenth-century virtuosi, and later adopted by Andrés Segovia (1893–1987) and almost all subsequent classical performers. Other famous guitarists, including Fernando Sor (1778–1839) and Francisco Tárrega (1852–1909), struck the strings with their fingertips. Players of steel-strung guitars utilize a wider variety of fingerstyle techniques; some play with only one or two right-hand fingers, or with *fingerpicks*; others use the little finger as well as the other digits.

finial   Ornamental feature on the top of a guitar *headstock*.

flat-top guitar   Steel-strung guitar with a flat (i.e. not arched) *top*, and played either *fingerstyle*, or with a *plectrum*.

fret   Originally, a loop of gut tied around the instrument's neck; now a metal ridge inset across the *fingerboard*. Holding down a *string* behind a fret causes the string to be pressed against it, raising the pitch. Frets are positioned on the neck at intervals of a semitone.

friction peg   Simple wooden tuning peg mounted vertically through a hole in the guitar's *headstock*. Friction pegs are found on many earlier guitars, and are also common on modern flamenco models. Unlike *machine heads*, they have no gears to facilitate their adjustment.

golpeadores   "Tap-plates" glued onto the *top* of flamenco guitars to protect the instrument's finish from the impact of the player's striking hand.

harmonic bar   Internal strut used to strengthen top or back of guitar.

harp-guitar   Steel-strung guitar with additional unfretted bass *strings* providing extended range. Developed by a number of late nineteenth-/early twentieth-century *luthiers*, notably Orville Gibson (1856–1918) (see Chapter Three).

Hawaiian guitar   Steel-strung guitar designed to be played in a horizontal position on the performer's lap. Notes and chords are formed using a metal bar instead of the fingers of the fretting hand, permitting the characteristic glissandi associated with Hawaiian guitar styles. The instrument's *action* is higher than a standard guitar's, and its neck profile is frequently square. See *Spanish guitar*.

headstock   Section of guitar neck above the *nut*. The *machine heads* or *friction pegs* are mounted on it.

heptachord   Seven-string guitar of the type used by Napoléon Coste (1806–1883) (see pages 36-7).

humbucker, humbucking pickup   Electro-magnetic transducer mounted under the *strings* of *archtop* and *flat-top* guitars. As the instrument's strings are struck, they create variations in the pickup's magnetic field and generate electrical currents; these can be amplified and fed to loud-speakers. Humbucking pickups are fitted with double magnetic coils, which increase output and help to suppress ("buck") hum and noise. They produce a distinctive, warm "electric guitar" sound, with more coloration and character than *piezo-electric pickups*.

Jumbo   Large-bodied, *flat-top acoustic guitar* design first introduced by the Gibson company in 1954 as a competitor to Martin's *Dreadnought*. Jumbo-style instruments have subsequently been produced by many other *luthiers*.

laminate   Material made by bonding together two or more thin sheets of different woods or other constituents. Laminates are often used in the construction of less expensive *acoustic guitars*, although *luthiers* favor solid woods for their finest instruments.

lutherie   The practice of making guitars and other stringed instruments.

luthier   Maker of stringed musical instruments, including guitars, violins, and lutes (the term is derived from the French word "luth").

Lyrachord   Carbon-fiber material developed and used by the Kaman company for the backs of their Ovation guitars.

lyre-guitar   Hybrid instrument, briefly popular in late eighteenth and early nineteenth centuries, with features borrowed from the guitar and the ancient Greek lyre. See pages 36-7 for illustration and description.

machine head, tuning machine   Geared tuning mechanism mounted horizontally (in *classical* and some *flat-top* designs) or vertically (in the majority of flat-tops and almost all *archtops*) in the guitar's *headstock*. It offers more stable and precise string adjustment than *friction pegs*.

mustache bridge   *Bridge* with long, upwardly curled ends.

nut   Block of bone, ivory, ebony, or synthetic material mounted at the *headstock* end of the neck. It sets the height and position of the *strings* as they pass through the grooved slots cut into its top, and also acts like a *fret*, defining the start of the vibrating length of each open string (see *bridge*).

pick   See *plectrum*.

pickguard, scratchplate   Protective plate of plastic, tortoiseshell, or other material, glued to the *tops* of *flat-top* guitars, or suspended (just below string height) above the *tables* of archtops. It is designed to protect the instrument's finish from damage by stray *plectrum* strokes.

piezo-electric pickup, bug   A transducer that converts vibrations from a guitar body or *bridge* into electrical currents which can then be amplified and fed to loudspeakers. Piezo-electric pickups provide a cleaner, more uncolored sound than *humbuckers* and other electro-magnetic units; they are now frequently fitted to *acoustic guitars* designed for use onstage.

pin bridge   Bridge of the type fitted to some eighteenth- and nineteenth-century guitars, and now almost universally used for steel-strung *flat-tops*. It incorporates holes into which the string ends are inserted; a wooden or ivory pin is then pushed into each hole, holding the string firm.

plectrum, pick   Thin, pointed piece of plastic, tortoise-shell, or other material, held between the thumb and forefinger of a guitarist's striking hand and used to pick or strum the instrument's *strings*.

punteado Spanish term for "plucking" style of guitar playing (cf *rasgueado*).

purfling See *binding*.

rasgueado Spanish term for "strumming" style of guitar playing (cf *punteado*).

re-entrant tuning Method of tuning on early guitars in which the highest or lowest pitches are found on the instrument's middle *courses*. This creates inversions in chordal playing and other distinctive effects.

resonator guitar Steel-strung guitar fitted with one or more metal resonator assemblies. These were developed by John Dopyera (1893–1988) to boost volume, but they also impart a distinctive tone-color which is especially popular with blues and country music players. See *Dobro*.

rose Parchment decoration mounted across/inside the *soundholes* of early guitars.

rosette Decorative inlay/design surrounding the *soundhole* on more recent *classical* and *flat-top* guitars.

saddle Sliver of bone, ivory, or synthetic material, mounted on the *bridge* of the guitar at the point where the *strings* pass across it. *Classical* and some *flat-top* guitars have a single saddle for all six strings; other flat-top designs, like those of the Lowden company (see pages 132-3 and 136-7) use split saddles to allow precise modification of string height and intonation. Many *archtop* bridges feature individually adjustable saddles for each string.

scratchplate See *pickguard*

semi-acoustic guitar A guitar fitted with one or more electro-magnetic pickups, but also featuring a hollow body and some degree of acoustic sound.

soundhole Hole cut into an acoustic guitar's *top* to help project its sound. *Classical* and *flat-top* models have a single round (or occasionally oval) soundhole, usually positioned near the center of the top and directly below the end of the *fingerboard*. *Archtop* designs have two *f-holes* carved into the center-left and center-right of their tops. Modern *luthiers* have experimented with re-positioning and re-sizing soundholes in order to improve the tone and projection of their instruments.

Spanish guitar i) Synonym for *classical guitar*.
ii) Term used by some twentieth-century American *luthiers* to describe any steel-strung guitar designed to be played in the "traditional" position (i.e. held upright in the arms). Spanish guitars are thus differentiated from *Hawaiian guitars*, which are placed horizontally on the performer's lap and fretted with a metal bar.

staff notation Standard method of writing music using one or more five-line staves. Guitar music is written, an octave higher than it sounds, on a single stave with a treble clef.

strings Early guitars – with the exception of *chitarre battenti* – were strung with gut, which continued to be used for Torres-style *classical* instruments until the 1940s, when nylon strings were introduced. Nylon provides greater durability and superior tone, and has now been adopted by nearly all classical and flamenco players. Steel strings began to be used by non-classical players in the late nineteenth century; their greater tension and differing tonal qualities required substantial changes in guitar design, and the modern *archtop* and *flat-top* guitar evolved in response to this.

tablature (tab) Means of writing down music for fretted instruments using one horizontal line to represent each string. Numbers corresponding to *frets* are superimposed on the lines, showing the finger positions needed to play each note and chord.

table See *top*.

tailpiece Metal or wooden fitting, positioned at the bottom edge of an *archtop* guitar's *table*, and acting as an anchor for the *string* ends. (Also used on some *flat-top* guitars.)

top, table The "face" of the guitar; its wooden top, with rounded or f-shaped *soundhole(s)* carved out of it, and the instrument's *bridge* mounted on it. It is glued into position, and braced on its underside.
See *table*.

tornavoz Brass or steel cone attached to the *soundhole* of some *classical guitars*, and intended to focus and project the sound of the instrument. Possibly invented by Antonio de Torres (1817–1892) (see page 43 for an example).

tricone *Resonator guitar* fitted with three resonator units.

truss-rod Metal bar inserted into the neck of a steel-strung guitar to improve its strength and rigidity. Many instruments have adjustable truss-rods whose tension can be changed to correct bowing or warping in the neck. Truss-rods are not found on *classical guitars*, whose gut or nylon *strings* exert much less pressure on their necks.

tuning machine See *machine head*.

vihuela The guitar's immediate ancestor, especially popular in Spain during the fifteenth and sixteenth centuries.

villanelle Sixteenth-/seventeenth-century popular song form thought to have originated in Naples, and frequently accompanied by the guitar (see page 22).

waist The narrowest part of the guitar's body, where its two sides slope inwards before extending to form the instrument's lower *bout*.

X-bracing Method of strengthening the *tops* of guitars and controlling/modifying their tonal characteristics by using struts configured in an "X" pattern (see pages 82 and 92 for further details). It was first popularized by C.F. Martin Sr. (1786-1873), and later became a standard method of bracing for *flat-top* and many *archtop* designs.

Bibliography and Discography

Achard, Ken: *The History and Development of the American Guitar*, Musical New Services Ltd., 1979

Bacon, Tony: *The Ultimate Guitar Book*, Dorling Kindersley, 1991

Benedetto, Robert: *Making an Archtop Guitar*, Centerstream, 1994

Bone, Philip J.: *The Guitar & Mandolin* (second edition), Schott, 1954

Brozman, Bob: *The History and Artistry of National Resonator Instruments*, Centerstream, 1993

Carter, Walter: *The Martin Book*, Balafon, 1995

Charters, Samuel B.: *The Bluesmen*, Oak Publications, 1967

Chase, Gilbert: *The Music of Spain* (second, revised edition), Dover Publications, 1959

Chinery, Scott & Bacon, Tony: *The Chinery Collection – 150 Years of American Guitars*, Balafon/Miller Freeman, 1996

Clinton, George: *Andrés Segovia*, Musical New Services, 1978

Denyer, Ralph: *The Guitar Handbook*, Pan, 1982

Donington, Robert: *The Interpretation of Early Music*, Faber & Faber, 1989

Evans, Tom & Mary Anne: *Guitars from the Renaissance to Rock*, Oxford University Press, 1977

Gruhn, George, & Carter, Walter: *Acoustic Guitars and other Fretted Instruments*, GPI Books, 1993

Gruhn, George, & Carter, Walter: *Gruhn's Guide to Vintage Guitars*, GPI Books, 1991

Grunfeld, Frederic V.: *The Art and Times of the Guitar*, Da Capo, 1974

Huber, John: *The Development of the Modern Guitar*, The Bold Strummer Ltd., 1994

Kernfeld, Barry (ed.): *The New Grove Dictionary of Jazz*, Macmillan, 1988

Longworth, Mike: *Martin Guitars, A History*, 4 Maples Press Inc., 1988

Morrish, John (ed.): *The Classical Guitar – A Complete History*, Balafon, 1997

Myers, Arnold (ed.): *Historic Musical Instruments in the Edinburgh University Collection*, (Catalogue, Vols. 1 & 2)

Pulver, Jeffrey, *A Biographical Dictionary of Old English Music*, Kegan Paul, Trench, Trubner & Co Ltd, 1927

Romanillos, José L.: *Antonio de Torres, Guitar Maker – His Life and Work*, Nadder/Element Books, 1987

Sadie, Stanley (ed.): *The New Grove Dictionary of Music and Musicians*, Macmillan, 1980

Scholes, Percy A.: *The Oxford Companion to Music (tenth edition)*, Oxford University Press, 1970

Segovia, Andrés: *An Autobiography of the Years 1893-1920*, Marion Boyars, 1977

Stimpson, Michael (ed.): *The Guitar – A Guide for Students and Teachers*, Oxford University Press, 1988

Summerfield, Maurice J.: *The Jazz Guitar* (third edition), Ashley Mark, 1993

Turnbull, Harvey: *The Guitar from the Renaissance to the Present Day*, Batsford, 1974

Tyler, James: *The Early Guitar*, Oxford University Press, 1980

Urlik, Sheldon: *A Collection of Fine Spanish Guitars from Torres to the Present*, Sunny Knoll Publishing Company, 1997

Various: *La Guitarra Española/The Spanish Guitar*, Opera Tres, 1993

Wade, Graham: *Traditions of the Classical Guitar*, Calder, 1980

Whitford, Eldon, Vinopal, David, & Erlewine, Dan: *Gibson's Fabulous Flat-Top Guitars*, GPI/Miller Freeman, 1994

DISCOGRAPHY

This selective discography lists CD recordings featuring some of the guitar models illustrated in this book. It is organized by section and chapter.

Section One: The Guitar's European Heritage

Few of the instruments shown in the first two chapters of this book are still in playable condition, and musicians wishing to recreate the sound of the five-course guitar and its eighteenth- and nineteenth-century successors are often obliged to use replicas made by modern luthiers. One remarkable exception to this general rule is Nigel North's *Guitar Collection* (Amon Ra, 1984), which features a variety of music played on original instruments, including guitars by Diaz (see pages 16-17), Fabricatore (see pages 30-31), and Panormo (see pages 34-37).

In the 1970s, guitarist, lutenist, and early music scholar James Tyler recorded a number of pioneering LPs featuring the "baroque" (5-course) guitar, as well as lute, archlute, and other instruments. These have now been reissued as budget-priced CDs.

Music for Merchants and Monarchs (Saga, 1976) includes works by Giovanni Paolo Foscarini (see page 18) and another seventeenth-century composer, Carlo Calvi. Other important records by Tyler are *Music of the Renaissance Virtuosi*, which contains a suite by Francesco Corbetta (see pages 18-22); and *The Early Guitar* (both on Saga).

Also of interest:

An Excess of Pleasure by the Palladian Ensemble (Linn, 1993) – which includes seventeenth-century solo and consort music featuring the group's guitarist and lutenist William Carter; *Music of Sor, Coste and Regondi* by David Starobin (GHA, 1996) – this features works by some of the most influential guitarist/composers of the nineteenth century. Starobin owns and uses guitars by C.F. Martin Sr. (see pages 48-9) and René François Lacôte (see pages 34-5); he also plays instruments by British luthier Gary Southwell (see pages 144-5).

Section Two: Twentieth-Century Developments
Chapters 3 and 4

Martin Taylor and David Grisman's *Tone Poems II* (Acoustic Disc, 1995) includes tracks on which Martin Taylor plays a Gibson Style "U" harp guitar (pages 52-3); a Gibson L-4 (pages 56-7); a Gibson L-5 (pages 58-9); a Gibson Super 400 (pages 60-61); the 1935 Epiphone De Luxe shown on pages 62-3; a D'Angelico Excel (pages 66-7); a D'Aquisto New Yorker (pages 68-9); and a Monteleone Radio Flyer (see pages 70-1).

Among the important "historical" recordings of guitars from this section are:
i) The compilation CD, *Pioneers of the Jazz Guitar* (Yazoo), which features classic duets by Eddie Lang and Lonnie Johnson, music by Lang and Joe Venuti (see pages 58-9), and tracks by Nick Lucas (pages 86-7).
ii) *When the Roses Bloom in Dixieland – The Complete Victor Recordings 1929-30* by the Carter Family (Rounder). Archtop guitars are not only used by jazz players; this compilation by the "first family" of American country music features Maybelle Carter (Johnny Cash's mother-in-law) playing her Gibson L-5.

Guitars by Robert Benedetto (see pages 72-5) are used by many leading soloists:
Bucky and John Pizzarelli – *The Complete Guitar Duos* (Stash, 1991); Howard Alden, Jimmy Bruno & Frank Vignola – *Concord Jazz Guitar Collective* (Concord, 1995); Gerry Beaudoin Trio – *Live At the Rendezvous* (Francesca, 1996); Ron Eschete Trio – *Soft Winds* (Concord, 1996); Jack Wilkins – *Mexico* (CTI, 1992); Adrian Ingram – on *The Ben Crosland Quintet* (Jazz Cat, 1995); Jimmy Bruno (with Bobby Watson) – *Live at Birdland* (Concord, 1997). Martin Taylor plays a Benedetto Cremona on his album with Stéphane Grappelli, *Reunion* (Linn, 1993).

Martin Taylor's W.G. Barker guitar (pages 78-9) was his main working instrument for a number of years. It can be heard on these albums, all recorded with Stéphane Grappelli: *Stéphane Grappelli at the Winery* (Concord, 1981), *Stéphane Grappelli Vintage 1981* (Concord, 1981/1992), and Stéphane Grappelli and Toots Thielemans' *Bringing It Together* (Cymekob, 1984). Before Martin acquired it, the Barker was also used on Elvis Presley's "Love Me Tender" (*Essential Elvis Presley* – RCA compilation, 1986), and the soundtrack of the TV series "Batman" (*Television's Greatest Hits Vol. 1* – TVT).

Chapter 5

Martin flat-tops have been popular with thousands of folk, bluegrass, and country performers. Guitarist Lester Flatt (whose work with banjoist Earl Scruggs was immensely influential in bluegrass music and beyond) played a D-18 in the early 1950s, switching to a D-28 (see pages 80-81) for his later performances and recordings. Flatt and Scruggs can be heard on *The Golden Era 1950-5* (Rounder compilation, 1992). Folk music stars The Kingston Trio, whose 1958 hit single "Tom Dooley" is reissued with other classics by the group on *The Kingston Trio – Greatest Hits* (Curb compilation, 1990) used Martin instruments, and 000s, OMs, and Dreadnoughts were frequently featured on early recordings by singers such as Joan Baez, David Bromberg, Judy Collins, Tom Paxton and others.

Other folk and country singers used both Martins and Gibsons. In the sleeve notes for his CD, *American Recordings* (American, 1994), Johnny Cash mentions two of his favorite guitars from the 1960s: a Martin D-28 spray-painted black, and a red Gibson J-200 – both subsequently lost. On "American Recordings," Cash accompanies himself with a black D-28 made in 1969, which he describes as his favorite instrument.

In the early 1970s, country rockers like Crosby, Stills, Nash and Young built their instrumental sound around Martin acoustics. Martins are also featured prominently on recordings such as David Crosby's solo album *If I Could Only Remember My Name* (Atlantic, 1971) and *Workingman's Dead* by the Grateful Dead (Warner, 1970).

Martin OMs, 000s (pages 80-85), and similar designs by other flat-top makers are especially favored by fingerstylists and blues players. Key performers in these styles include Stefan Grossman, whose many fine records include *Yazoo Basin Boogie* (Shanachie, 1991); and Rory Block (*When a Woman Gets the Blues* – Rounder, 1995), who frequently uses Eric Schoenberg's Soloist model (see pages 98-9). Eric Clapton's acoustic guitar work is showcased on his *Unplugged* album (Reprise, 1992).

Gibson flat-tops have been used by many famous performers from the 1920s onwards. Mississippi Delta bluesman Robert Johnson (c.1912–1938) often used a Gibson L-1 (see page 86), and is seen playing one on the cover of his *Complete Recordings* (Columbia, 2 CD set). Gospel musician Rev. Gary Davis and his J-200 "Miss Gibson" (see pages 88-9 and 134-5) are featured on the classic album *Blind Gary Davis – Harlem Street Singer* (Prestige/Bluesville, 1960). The Everly Brothers played Southerner Jumbos (predecessors to the Country-Western model – see pages 88-9) on "Wake Up, Little Susie" and "Bye Bye Love" (*The Fabulous Everly Brothers* – Ace; the record cover shows them with their distinctive "Everly Brothers" models – see page 135), while Elvis Presley was frequently photographed with a J-200. John Lennon and George Harrison used Gibson J160E electric Jumbos for many of the early Beatles recordings (*The Beatles – 1962-1966* – Apple, 2-CD set).

Later rock and country artists also favored Gibson flat-tops; Emmylou Harris uses a J-200 onstage, and her SJN Southerner Jumbo (see pages 88-9) can be heard on "Prayer in Open D" from her album *Cowgirl's Prayer* (Grapevine, 1994). Songwriter and rhythm guitarist John Hiatt is another Gibson devotee – although he also uses Taylor guitars for live performances and recordings.

Taylors (see pages 94-97) are the choice of many other contemporary flat-top players. Among them is Dan Crary, whose album *Jammed If I Do* (Sugar Hill, 1994) contains some superb acoustic guitar work from Crary and guests Tony Rice, Doc Watson (both closely associated with Santa Cruz instruments), and Beppe Gambetta. Leo Kottke's twelve-string Taylor is featured on his CD *Standing in My Shoes* (Private Music, 1997). Other high-profile Taylor players include former Paul McCartney sideman Laurence Juber, who makes use of a variety of models, including the Baby Taylor (illustrated on pages 142-3), on the CD *Groovemasters Volume 1* (Solid Air, 1997) and Rickie Lee Jones – who plays a Taylor 712 on her CD *Pop Pop* (Geffen, 1991).

Chapter 6

Django Reinhardt's recordings with his Selmer/Maccaferri guitars (see pages 108-109) have been reissued on a variety of different labels. Useful compilations include: *Django Reinhardt – Swing in Paris 1936-1940* (Affinity, 3-CD set); *Django Reinhardt Chronological Vol. 1* (JSP); *Swinging With Django* (Happy Days); and *Souvenirs* (Decca).

Chapter 7

Performer and writer Bob Brozman is the leading expert on the history and development of the resonator guitar. He uses original pre-war Nationals and, on his more recent recordings, instruments from National Reso-Phonic. Brozman's many fine CDs include *Blue Hula Stomp* (Fantasy/Kicking Mule, 1981); *Devil's Slide* (Rounder, 1988); and *A Truckload of Blues* (Rounder, 1991).

Nationals can also be heard on recordings by Roy Book Binder (*Bookeroo!* – Rounder, 1988), Keb' Mo' (*Just Like You* – OKeh-Epic, 1996) and Corey Harris (*Between Midnight and Day* – Alligator, 1995).

Chapter 8

Andrés Segovia's groundbreaking performances are essential listening for anyone interested in the development of the modern classical guitar. EMI's double-CD boxed set, *The Art of Segovia: the HMV Recordings 1927-39* – EMI, 1989, covers the period when he was using guitars by Hernández and Hauser (see pages 124-125), and includes his interpretations of works by De Visée, J.S. Bach, Tárrega, Ponce, and others.

Julian Bream's distinguished musical career is well documented on record. Most of the albums he made for the RCA label from the 1960s onwards are now reissued as BMG CDs, and his recent recordings, frequently featuring Hauser guitars, appear on EMI. Notable examples of these include *Nocturnal* (EMI, 1994) with music by Britten, Lutoslawski, and others – and *Sonata* (EMI, 1995)

Bream's friend and fellow guitar virtuoso John Williams has favored instruments by Fleta (see pages 126-127) and, latterly, the Australian luthier Greg Smallman. Williams' many fine recordings can be found on the Columbia and Sony labels: among them are *The Spirit of the Guitar* (Sony, 1989), which includes music by Ponce, Villa-Lobos ,and Barrios; and *The Baroque Album* (Sony, 1989), featuring works by Telemann, Scarlatti, and others.

Other devotees of Fleta instruments include Turibio Santos and Carlos Bonell, while American guitarist Eliot Fisk uses a 1986 "Fleta e hijos" for his CD recital *Guitar Fantasia* (Musicmasters, 1989), and frequently performs with a 1988 Thomas Humphrey Millennium guitar (see pages 128-129).

Section Three: Today and Tomorrow

Chapter 9

Lowden guitars (pages 92-93 and 136-137) can be heard on recent CDs by British singer-songwriter Richard Thompson. They are also favorites of John Jennings, guitarist with singer-songwriter Mary Chapin Carpenter, and are featured on her album *A Place in the World* (Columbia, 1996). On the same CD, John Jennings makes use of a Martin Backpacker (see pages 142-143).

Ovation users (see pages 138-139) include Al DiMeola, whose many outstanding recordings include the classic *Friday Night in San Francisco*, recorded live in 1980 with John McLaughlin and Paco De Lucia, and now reissued on a Columbia Legacy CD; Adrian Legg (*Waiting For a Dancer* – Red House, 1997); and the late Marcel Dadi (*Country Guitar Flavors* – EPM, 1992). Dadi also used Taylor guitars.

Gary Southwell's Series A guitar (pages 144-145) is featured on David Starobin's *Newdance Vol. 1* (Bridge). Southwell guitars can also be heard on *Night Birds* by the Danish Guitar Trio (Point) and *Renaissance and Celtic Music* by James Kline (Chamber).

Martin Taylor's Yamaha AEX 1500 (pages 146-147) is featured on his *Portraits* album (Linn, 1996); he played the first prototype model of this guitar on *Artistry* (Linn, 1992).

Fingerstyle jazz player Earl Klugh has used Paul McGill resonator guitars and classical guitars (see pages 148-149) since 1988. They can be heard on his album *A Sudden Burst of Energy* (Warner, 1996).

Index